Home to the HOMESTEAD

In this novel by

Richard Everett Londgren

entrepreneur

Krag Jensen

moves to the Iowa
HOMESTEAD
of his Danish great-
grandfather, where
Krag had enjoyed
summer visits as a kid
from Chicago.

Author
Richard Everett Londgren
relaxes after operating his
Chandler & Price
platen press.

© 2015

Foreword

To the best of my knowledge, my grandfathers didn't benefit from the Homestead Act of free land when they came to the United States from Sweden. But they were skilled craftsmen and farmers, so by wit and grit, they did develop significant Homesteads, such as Grandfather Londgren's 'homestead' as shown in the cover photo.

Much of the Saga of my grandparents remains a mystery to me, but it has served as a seed for this story. As in typical fiction, that seed sprouted with nourishment from imagination and exaggeration—including my references to the Homestead Act.

No doubt my imagination in this story goes far beyond what my grandparents might have even dreamed about.

Still, I thank them. My vague recollections and the actual photo here serve as the foundation for this Homestead story.

Richard Everett Londgren

Contents

Chapter 1: On the Air

"Listen up, Folks! This is Jim Stardad of KRRL. We've got a new local program right here at your own station KRRL! As you know, that stands for K-rural here in Iowa. Certainly fits our discussion today.

"And here in our studio to host this discussion is Krag Jensen. So, tell us, Krag, about yourself, why you're starting this radio program, and who the others are."

"Glad to! And thanks for the air time, Jim.

"When I was a kid in Chicago, I used to come here in Iowa during the summer to visit my grandparents. Recently, my brothers and sister and I inherited the farm. Because our parents are dead, the place passed on to us. None of us wanted to farm, so we decided to sell all the land—except the homestead. With a reasonable financial arrangement, the others were glad to turn that over to me.

"I was the youngest and loved to visit here in the summers. Got to know and respect our grandfather. The others in our clan evidently didn't share that feeling. Guess Grandfather had mellowed by my time. All of us, at least, did love our grandmother.

"So I hope to restore the place, including Grandfather's Ford and Fordson tractors. That's why I recruited this local all-star support team. Your listeners probably know them.

"We'll need Harry Hansen and his hardware store, for sure!"

That's me! If we ain't got it, it doesn't exist," interjected Harry. "Happy to be on Krag's team!"

"Next," added Krag, "here's Mike Miller, our ace mechanic."

"Yeah, watch me try to get Krag's Fordson running. Way older than I am," laughed Mike.

"Last but not least," added Krag, "our retired shop teacher, Steve Swanson. Think you can shape up our shop, Steve?"

"Should be duck soup after teaching the kids," answered Steve. "Guess the school board gave up on them—and me. So they shut the shop down and offered it all—plus me—to Krag. Now, no telling what we'll run into with the buildings and a mish-mash of that old shop equipment—and me as foreman. Should be interesting, though!"

"Next time," said Krag, to conclude the introduction to the new program, "we'll start with information about the term 'Homestead.' What it means in history, in the distribution of land in the USA, and what it means to families. And to our exploration of the challenge of change in life today.

"Now it's back to you, Jim," said Krag.

Bishop Grundtvig

"We look forward to your ongoing reports," Jim responded. "Your place, Krag, has become sort of an icon in our community. We think lots of our listeners will be curious about your progress and how it fits in our community of Grundtvig. And that name alone should be

worth another of your programs, because it emphasizes the tradition of the Danish folk schools as fostered in Denmark by N.F.S. Grundtvig, who was an educator as well as pastor and church musician.

"Sorry to say, his name doesn't trip off the tongue smoothly for radio broadcasting. Good reason, I suppose, why most folks here just refer to our community as Grund. Lends itself to slogans such as 'Go Grund!' Or at school, 'back to the daily Grund!' Maybe a merchant promoting a 'Grund Opening'!"

"Bishop Grundtvig would probably have appreciated that nickname," chuckled Krag. "After all, to the dismay of the Danish elite, he saw himself as part of the practical working class and wanted those folks to have a chance at schooling."

"Seems like a good time to sign off, before the play on words gets worse," Jim then announced. "As for this program," he continued, "we hope it provides a 'Grund time for all'.

"So ya'll come back now, ya hear!"

With that, Krag and his team groaned and laughed with Jim.

Chapter 2: Homestead Renewal

As the "Homestead Team" met to plan the restoration of the property created by Krag's grandfather, they did talk about the significance of the term "Homestead." They discussed the prairie sense of the word when Krag showed a reproduction of "The Homestead" as painted by John Stuart Curry for the Interior Department in 1938.

"A long way from the Homesteads of the aristocrats of England," laughed Krag. "Surprising, isn't it, how many of those English traditions still inspire us here in the Colonies."

"That family scene warms my heart," said Steve. "We don't have that togetherness of purpose these days it seems."

The Homestead by John Stuart Curry

"Quite a contrast to your *Homestead*, Krag," stated Mike. "Good reminder about the work and determination that helped us advance to our farms and communities of today."

"Reminds me about the loss of some of that togetherness in my family," explained Krag, as he told of his family conflict

about the settlement of the estate. "Lot of emotional baggage related to this farm, to our parents, even to the feeling my sibs seem to have that I was favored in some way.

"Maybe I did have advantages—but not necessarily because I got special favors while growing up. More like the luck of heredity. And led to special opportunities."

"Oh yeah," said Harry, "we, along with the most of the community, it seems, figure you're well off. Rich, as a matter of fact, and that's why you can restore your *Homestead*. Probably will cost a bundle!"

"I certainly can afford it," admitted Krag.

"I'd be curious to hear your story, not just the rumors that float around," said Mike. "As a struggling businessman, I certainly commend you for what you've achieved!"

"Let's use a future broadcast to feature my story. Give me time to boil it down for our listeners—and you, of course. But for now, let me thank you again for agreeing to participate in renewing my *Homestead*," Krag responded. "I didn't select you by random. And not just because of your special knowledge, but also because I recalled my good feelings about you from my summers with Grandfather. I liked your helpfulness and friendliness then, and I sense it now.

"By the way, when you agreed to joining my team, you didn't ask and I didn't tell about pay for your participation. But like the board of directors of companies I've been associated with, you deserve compensation for your commitment. So we can work out those financial details later.

Meanwhile, I hope this can be a family affair, with your families involved to the extent they want to be."

"I think I can speak for Mike and Steve," said Harry, "that we talked it over and we simply like the spirit and challenge of your project. And we didn't even think of personal payment. And, yes, our families are already excited about your *Homestead* project—and feel honored to be involved."

"Speaking of family," interjected Steve, "we have been saddened not just about the not-unusual strife in your family, but about the tragedy that took the lives of your wife and son and daughter. KRRL and our newspaper reported extensively about your terrible loss."

"As you know," started Krag, as he wiped away a tear, "a freak accident that couldn't be avoided. Their plane came in to O'Hare just when a tornado hit. Instead of just being buffeted by a typical thunderstorm, the plane was blown off the runway into a steel tower and exploded. It's been two years, and it haunts me continually.

"All the more tragic that they were returning from visiting her family in Denmark," he said, followed by a solemn pause....

"You probably know that I first met Christine when our family visited Denmark. Then she and I got acquainted and fell in love while we were both students at the University of Chicago."

"So very sorry!" muttered Mike.

"Now I hope this project helps me move on—or at least beyond the immediate past. Back to the happy times I had

here as a kid, learning from Grandfather. Swimming, flirting, softball, the Fourth, biking, roller-skating.

"And learning to drive, first on Grandfather's cherished Fordson, then on his Model T and A. Later on his Ford tractor. I learned from him as we worked together to plan and repair and build. He listened to my ideas too, and we both enjoyed discussing them and testing them. Sometimes in friendly arguments. I got a sense of his interest in design, which showed up in his matching barn and granary, including the graceful curved rafters he created.

"In some ways, Grandfather identified with Henry Ford, who hated farming in the old way and hoped his tractor would make rural life easier. And that went for his Model T, suited to a rugged life as well. And known as the Tin Lizzie, the 'faithful servant.'

"So now, here we are again, as in my summer visits, exploring ideas about building and repairing. Thanks for helping me cope and carry on.

"I hope to visit here regularly," explained Krag. "A good shot on the highway from Chicago. The distance would be easy by plane, but so far I can't deal with my personal emotions. Gave up on my long-ago intent to buy and fly my own plane. Still distraught about flying. Maybe I will at least be able to fly out of Midway someday, avoiding the sad memory of O'Hare."

"Count on us to help you in any way we can," said Mike. "Train connections aren't bad. And we could even pick you up in Chicago. Give us time to plan as we cruise west."

"Thanks for your thoughtfulness," murmured Krag. "I'm eager to repair and rebuild the *Homestead*. Should help distract me from myself."

"We look forward to knowing you at this later stage in your life," said Harry. "See if you still have that zest for the challenge of new ideas that you demonstrated years ago when you stayed with your grandfather. You sure did seem like a chip off the old block then...and now, we hope."

Chapter 3: Homestead History

In preparation for their next radio presentation, the *Homestead* team decided they needed to do some research.

Krag had gone back to Chicago and had returned. "Not so bad," he declared about the drive. "Great fall weather, interesting harvest scenes. Intriguing to see football players practicing as I drove through small towns. Also, got some old-fashioned home-cooking at a restaurant or two along the way.

"Reminds me, Mike, that you mentioned that I might camp out in a Winnebago while we work on the buildings here. I thought about that and agree that could be just the ticket, especially when we take on the restoration of the home of FarFar and FarMor. The motorhome might provide fun later for exploring the area, too.

"Maybe we could drive my car up to Forest City so I can get a motorhome right from the factory."

"Let's do it!" Mike responded. "I know the Hansons who make the Winnebago rigs, and I think they would find our project intriguing. Mention it on our radio program too. Good promotion for them and us."

"Maybe we could all go," Steve suggested.

"And we could tow your car behind your new Winnebago when we head back," said Harry.

"Good time to plan while traveling to figure out just what we want to talk about in our next radio session," said Krag. "I think we should share background information about the 'Homestead Act' and how that relates to our project."

"Sounds like a good foundation about that could carry over into later programs," agreed Steve. "Might generate some audience response, too, if some listeners have a family link to the 'Homestead Act'. Might help promote discussions in high school and college classes too."

For their first research stop, they checked in at the regional library serving surrounding schools and communities.

In the library, the research assistant welcomed them. They admitted only rudimentary understanding of the U.S Homestead Act. Rusty about what they had learned in school long ago. But they declared that they had heard that the rich farmland of Iowa had been a prime plum to be picked as part of that Act.

As their "tutor" plied them with information and questions, they learned that the English legacy impacted the early distribution of land in the United States. From the time of President Thomas Jefferson, the Northern states encouraged the idea of the "yeoman farmer." So the Free Soil Party of 1848 took up the cause till the 1850s, and then the Republican Party demanded that the new lands of the West be made available to farmers rather than wealthy planters.

Opposition came from the South, but after those states seceded, Congress passed the initial Homestead Act of 1862, signed by President Abraham Lincoln, in which public land in the West was granted to any U.S. male citizen of at least age 21 or younger or head of household. He had to be willing to settle on and farm a grant of about 160 acres for at least five years, plus making improvements.

"In a way, my great-grandfather got lucky and benefited from that opportunity," said Krag. "He came as an immigrant from Denmark at the time of the Civil War and was recruited for the Union Army. Lucky to survive, to start with. Then that Army service earned him immediate citizenship, which later qualified him for a land grant. He displayed both of those documents in the room he used as an office, and now I have those to put in my office. And his Army discharge, too, as a reminder of how lucky he was to survive the war without injury.

"He saved his meager military pay and eventually invested in more of this rich Iowa land.

"And now," Krag continued, "his land that started with the Homestead Act has become my own *Homestead*."

The other three on the team conceded that none of their ancestors had been able to get such a grant. Then because of the rising value of Iowa land, costs exceeded what their families could afford anyway, so they turned to other occupations.

But they agreed that they were happy to share in Krag's *Homestead* challenge.

By the time of their next radio session, they felt they had learned about and discussed the Homestead Act enough to ad lib their way through the program. But for a bit of insurance, Krag had prepared duplicate sets of cards indicating who might respond about which topic.

Back at the radio station, Jim welcomed them with a warm greeting—and a big grin. "Seems like your first session generated a good response. That's what we like to hear, of course," he chortled.

"Anyway, we compiled some questions that came from our listeners, so you can work them in if appropriate during a future program. And maybe we'll get some more responses after today.

"The topic you mentioned sounds good. Even I want to learn about the Homestead Act. Before you go on, I just want to wish you well—and remind you to keep up the banter that makes your discussion lively."

They did. While they shared information, they kidded each other about doing the research at the library. About their rolling conference room in the Winnebago, and about the luck of the draw that made Krag a winner and left the other three out of the free land.

Then they invited listeners to call in to the station with Homestead stories and with questions about the impact of the Homestead Acts.

Before they left the station, they learned that several callers had already responded.

"I'll have those typed up for you," said Jim. "Looks like we've got a winner. See you next month. Same place on your radio dial," Jim added, with another chortle.

Chapter 4: Krag's Success Story

The fresh challenge of restoring his *Homestead* pushed Krag into activity and regenerated past enthusiasm. Ever since he spent summers with his Grandfather Jensen, he had responded to his grandfather's creativeness and determination, as he experimented with electricity and plumbing—though he wasn't inspired when asked because he was small to crawl in and clean out the cistern. Though Grandfather hadn't gone to college, he had benefited from workshops and trade shows sponsored by farm organizations. And he read how-to-do-it magazines. He also pestered mechanics at Mike's garage for help. Even sought information from high school students interested in cars and motorcycles.

Though Krag acknowledged that the business knowledge of his parents and sibs required skill and talent, he didn't lean toward that kind of creativeness. He did, however, find his sibs to be highly valuable advisors later in his own ventures, such as helping him defend his patents.

As with much of the country, the Great Depression sidetracked his family, even in the affluent Oak Park suburb of Chicago. Their jobs continued, barely, but their investments didn't.

Based on his bent toward science and his experiments in electronics, Krag had wangled a scholarship to the University of Chicago. Through creative 'matriculation', he expanded that scholarship into an opportunity for advanced study in Denmark. There he focused on the theories of Hans Christian Orsted, a Danish physicist and chemist who discovered that electric currents create magnetic fields, therefore an important aspect of electromagnetism.

Besides being intrigued by the Danish scientist, Krag found a personal parallel when he learned that the Danish Nobel-Prize-winner in science lived about the same time as Krag's great-grandfather Jens, who had left Denmark and eventually acquired his land in Iowa through the U.S. Homestead Act. And Krag learned of another surprise in connection with the Danish scientist: he had become a close friend of the Danish storyteller Hans Christian Andersen. What a contrast in interests! Krag had thought.

Then, when the Nazis loomed over Denmark, Krag scurried back to the U.S. And into the Navy, where he continued his college education in the Navy V-12 program—at the University of Chicago. He reflected later about the contrast in developments there: While he was tinkering with basic electronics, the Manhattan Project to develop the atom bomb was also moving desperately on at the University. He had heard that some type of primitive computer had been created and was helping with the complicated calculations involved.

At the same time too, several Danish students had earlier enrolled at the University and were locked in the United States for the duration. Naturally, Krag connected with those students, in particular Christine Thorsen. Of course, he remembered her as attractive and vivacious. But he also found her to be smart and assertive—and lovable.

Krag mentioned to her the apparent contradiction of Orsted's scientific interest in contrast to his friendship with Hans Christian Andersen. Not so unusual, declared Christine. Like other Danish intellectuals, Orested delved into philosophy, she explained, as did another famous Danish scientist, Niels Henrik David Bohr. She mentioned that Bohr also happened to win a Nobel Prize for Physics.

Not all the Danish students subscribed to the peace-loving nature of the country. One had ancestry in a former section of Denmark called Holstein, now a part of Germany. Hans Schreiber did not like the attention Krag paid to Christine, so he plotted to defuse Krag's romantic advances with Christine. During an underwater exercise, he conspired to disconnect Krag's oxygen hose. But American "Frogmen" participating in the activity caught the "Holsteiner" and hauled him to the surface, while another rescued Krag.

In a Navy court-martial, the Holsteiner was ejected from the Navy program and sent to a work farm as a prisoner of war.

But before the prisoner was shipped out, the Frogmen took him for a boat ride on Lake Michigan. When well away from shore, the Frogmen dumped the prisoner overboard. And put a scare in him as they waved farewell. But a few minutes later, the Frogmen returned to check on the desperate, thrashing swimmer. Then, when signaled, Krag threw a life preserver attached to a long rope to the swimmer. After the detested Hans Schreiber grabbed on to the life preserver, the Frogman at the controls revved the engine and the boat surged forward, causing Schreiber to plow through and under the turbulent water, looking frenzied as he coughed and gushed water.

"Our version of the 'keel-hauling' of the past," grinned the Frogman.

Then they sent this "Danish-German" criminal to an enclosure with German prisoners of war, who didn't look kindly at a German claiming Danish citizenship so he could avoid the Nazi military and flee to America.

Back to normal in the Navy, Krag experimented with a variety of electronic applications that supported the guidance systems of ships—and even torpedoes. For the remainder of the war, he devised and tested a variety of instrumentations, sometimes on ships and in submarines in direct conflict with the enemy. And he learned what he could about the significance of the giant computers being used in support of secret wartime research.

After the war, he made further important connections, including courting Christine. That proved to be a major achievement in his life when she agreed to marry him. After the war, she concentrated on being a mother and homemaker, as Krag turned to industrial applications of his knowledge and talents.

Out of that commercial involvement, Krag's career included creative applications of electronics. But it also led to long dispute over his independent development of a product, apart from his career.

On his own, he had created a device that seemed simple, yet unique enough to earn a patent for him. And then it became the focus of an extended confrontation in the automobile industry, in particular. The conflict involved Krag's switch that enabled a parking light to turn off automatically after a short delay.

The first stage of his development featured a device containing mercury, in which the slight heat generated by a parking light would turn it off. Then, applying his knowledge of instruments, he changed his initial concept to a metallic heat sensor. Simpler, safer, less cost to produce. But still his patent.

When he began to publicize his parking-light applications, the device caught the fancy of the public. And the auto industry responded, as the patent battle began.

Ultimately, thanks to the support of Krag's family and a squad of patent specialists, Krag's side finally prevailed.

Later, when the dust settled, Krag laughed with Grandfather Jensen: "You might say I bet the farm!"

Ultimately, that device led to a variety of other applications in home and commercial lighting and related controls.

And led to a handsome—and ongoing—payoff for all involved.

But, as all knew, the financial gain couldn't begin to offset Krag's personal loss later, when Christine and their son Thor and daughter Jennifer died in the Chicago plane crash.

Chapter 5: Pondering the Possible

"The *Homestead* quartet," as they had become known from their broadcasts, continued to explore ideas to share in their monthly broadcasts.

Even when they talked about the important transition of horses to tractors, they generated reactions. And that feedback, such as old-timers regretting the demise of farm horses, became fuel for further commentary by the foursome—including some disagreement themselves.

When Mike told about tuning up the Krag's Fordson tractor, the program stirred up controversy about what brand of tractor was best. As Steve regaled his radio audience about the planned "artistic" refinishing of the Fordson, some listeners berated the gray of the Fordson, declaring that wasn't even a color. Not like their favorite green, red or yellow, depending on their machine of choice. Even women, of course, began to get in on the act, sharing their color preferences.

"Guess that means that it's time to bring your wives into the discussion," said Krag. "Household hints, cooking suggestions, nutrition, fashion—who knows what!"

Jim immediately ratified that idea, because he quickly grasped the significance of female buyers—and how that would appeal to more advertisers for KRRL.

The color discussion brought another surprising response. A representative of Deere & Company called to suggest the KRRL quartet come and take in the sea of green at their headquarters.

"It's just a hop, skip and jump away from you to get to Moline, Illinois."

"Sounds interesting, fun…but not that fast," chimed in Harry. "Could be part of a road trip with stops on the way."

And the others voted with him. "We'll say yes, but with winter waiting to attack, we'll wait till after the spring thaw next year. Maybe we can do some local visiting in towns and schools and churches in the meantime. Sort of test out our pitch locally.

"About time for me to move out of my Winnebago and into my house. Seems to be almost ship shape, thanks to the contractors and a bunch of volunteers. Good job coordinating all that, Steve!"

"For now," said Steve, "we improvised with the electricity for the house and other buildings. Your clever grandfather had installed a battery-powered low-voltage system with a gasoline-powered generator to charge the batteries. Seems good enough for now, but next year we'll connect with the rural electrification program. Lots more power in lots more places."

"Grandfather and I talked about that years ago," said Krag. "Got to hand it to him for innovations and for being willing to bet on improvements. His electrical project intrigued me and even motivated me to get in on the opportunities in electronics."

"Made you rich, too!" laughed Harry. "Don't know why I didn't think of your ideas. And how to make money with them."

"Well," said Krag, "here's another idea for us to think over and get reactions too while we're snowbound."

"Okay," responded Mike, "you've got my attention. What are you cooking up in that 'never-stop-thinking' brain of yours?

"I worry that the changes and challenges of rural life will ambush all of us one of these days," began Krag. "Towns, schools, churches, everything on the prairie is withering. More and more, big companies are calling the shots on what farmers can raise and how that can be processed. They control with patented seeds and monopolize the fertilizer. And determine how products are marketed.

"Even Wall Street would cringe at the risks and costs farmers face every season. Equipment, fuel, fertilizer, seed, insurance, taxes. Talk about a gamble!

"Perhaps the worst of all is the growing isolation of families.

"In looking at my own heritage, I see advantages to many Danish traditions of cooperation. This town of Grundtvig puts fresh focus on the Danish roots of my family and involves several Danish communities and residents of the area. Not to mention nearby Dana College, with that heritage too. And I'm pleased that the tradition of the Danish learning, fostered in Denmark by pastor and educator N.F.S Grundtvig, gets support here. Including a 'folk school' at several locations in our area. The namesake of our town would feel honored. My grandfather, who never stopped learning, endorsed this development and would be pleased with the progress too.

"Thanks to our location on Interstate 80 between two major cities, our community has grown steadily. Who would have predicted how a mall, for instance, and other consumer attractions might invigorate our town. Now I think we can lead the way in further development."

"I get your drift," said Harry. "I know there is nothing sure but death—oh, I'm sorry for being insensitive, Krag."

"That's okay," responded Krag. "Thanks largely to the distracting activity here and to the friendship of you and many others, I'm adjusting. And accepting reality. Anyway, as you were saying...."

"Besides taxes, change is a sure thing," added Harry.

"Yeah," said Krag, "I quote my forbearer, King Knute of Denmark. You can't stop the tide."

"Do you think Grund can become more of a center than it is now?" asked Mike.

"Maybe," speculated Krag. "Our location seems ideal. In the middle of smaller communities. Far enough from Des Moines on the east and Council Bluffs and Omaha on the west to develop as a regional focus. We could become a cultural and entertainment center, even bring more small schools together for better educational opportunities. Promote study of electronics, of course, including robotics. Provide advanced medical services. Perhaps a religious facility could serve the fragmented and failing congregations all around us. A museum could feature our past and present, while pointing to our future. Honor Iowans such as Herbert Hoover, John Wayne, Norman Borlaug, Glenn Miller and Bob Feller.

"And commercial progress would develop, of course."

"Maybe," inserted Steve, "we could become an entertainment center, like Branson, Missouri aims to be. We could bring in Lawrence Welk, add a production of Meredith Willson's *The Music Man* from Mason City, feature Glenn Miller's music."

"Deserves a lot of thought," pondered Harry. "We can seek input, test it out, get a mixture of reactions, even from our radio broadcasts."

"Guess we'll have to soft-pedal these ideas, so people don't dismiss them before we even define them," cautioned Krag.

"I admit," muttered Mike, "it does seem like 'pie in the sky, bye and bye', but most new ideas do, I suppose."

Chapter 6: Winter Solstice

Before winter blustered in, the KRRL quartet of prognosticators closed down Fall with comments about the just-finished football season. During Thanksgiving gatherings, they even got positive reactions from high school students about the constrained broadcast comments about the team. The players admitted that the Great Danes hadn't been all that Great. But wait till next year! they barked.

After referring to the current contestants, they harked back to their own playing days. And they agreed on one memory: November is too darn cold to play football...on frozen turf and sometimes in a snowstorm. Basketball in a warm gym looks like welcome relief.

So the quartet promised they would report on air about the basketball teams—boys and girls. Not necessarily in that order, because Iowa was noted for the outstanding competition among girls.

Delayed harvest earned commentary, about partly frozen ground in the cornfields. Stuck tractors. Plugged picking machines...but that risk still beats the old days of husking by hand.

On the air, they repeated a warning that farmers heard every Fall. Keep your hands far away from a running corn picking machine when you try to pull tangled corn stalks out of the corn picker. Unfortunately, they reminded listeners, every Fall seems to produce lost fingers, a hand and even an arm.

Then they heralded the annual relief: this year's harvest had finished before the first blizzard.

But the usual harvest contradiction appeared again: Great crop meant great price drop. The perennial peril of farming.

That tale of woe triggered the opening KRRL salvo about the steady change in life on the prairie. The quartet took turns in reporting what seemed like the obvious: big investment for risky return, big farms swallowing smaller ones, absentee owners, diversification fading, families leaving the soil, towns shrinking, crop choices constrained by corporations.

Guess that's enough for now, admitted the quartet. Let us know your reactions...and solutions, if you have any.

Almost immediately, Jim reported about phoned-in reactions. But darn few solutions. He promised to have the feedback typed for them, with hope for helpful commentary during the next program.

About a week later, they got feedback in another form. Krag ran into Jim, who was riffling through some mail at the post office. "Hey, Krag, responses to your show are growing. Take a look at this postcard. From a professor at Iowa State University."

The card began with "Hold your horses! You'll scare the pants off your listeners. We study change all the time to try to predict trends. Even our students, who think they can simply roll with the punches, are actually Nervous Nellies too!"

It was signed Kay Arnesen, PhD in the Department of Rural Economics.

"Well," declared Krag, "there's our next topic. But dare we even tippy-toe into the ideas about the types of consolidation we've discussed?"

Unfortunately, Christmas, the time usually dedicated to good will, generated other reactions when the quartet and their families talked with fellow parishioners at the Lutheran, Methodist and Catholic churches.

We don't need Scrooge on the radio to remind us of gloom and doom! That seemed to be the refrain that offset the usual good feeling of Christmas as well as hopes for the New Year.

So when the quartet gathered to lick their wounds, Krag offered a sour greeting: "Christmas response negative... and New Year grumpy!

"At least I will feel better when this Fordson comes to life again," Krag admitted as he and Mike continued on the restoration of the tractor. "Even some skinned knuckles will remind me that challenges often cause bruises."

"Cheer up!" said Mike. "Your old tractor will be worth the effort, and so will your crusade for our community."

When Steve and Harry dropped by, they listened sympathetically.

"Guess the professor will have the last laugh after all," admitted Steve.

"Hey," scoffed Mike, with a restrained grin, "who ever heard of a professor named Kay, anyway!"

"Oh," countered Harry with his half-grin, "there was that band leader, Kay Kyser and his Kollege of Musical Knowledge."

"Guess we'll just have to thank our professor for his warning," said Krag, "and only take baby steps toward change."

So, in their first broadcast of the New Year, they stressed how Grund could start serving the wider community by converting an abandoned warehouse into an entertainment center. For roller skating, dancing, concerts, movies, even lectures.

A couple of days later, Jim alerted them that they had hit the jackpot. Lots of listener responses, with thanks from merchants. Cards and letters, too, including another from the Iowa State professor, who wrote: "Good you're off your high horse. And remember, don't get the cart before the horse. Help the folks trot into the sunset, not gallop. Beware of horse manure. But keep on wrangling!" Kay Arnesen, PhD in Rural Economics, Iowa State University.

"Guess the professor likes his equine metaphor," responded Krag. "We should be able to get some fun out that, including our hope to convert a horse barn to show horse operas."

"Don't know if I like his smart-ass academic tone," said Mike. "Anyway, better than being ignored. Maybe we should challenge him to a shoot-out at O.K. Corral."

"Get that!" declared Krag. "Mike created a metaphor about a meeting we should try to arrange with the professor. We could jump into my Winnie and head toward Ames for an in-your-face confrontation.

"Okay, we'll throw down the gauntlet in our next program," laughed Krag. "At least we should have some fun during our crusade."

In the next postcard, the professor accepted the challenge. "I have my second groomed, so to speak. My students will be hanging over the corral fence. Not sure which side they'll be on. For the good of Iowa, let the joust begin!" Kay Arensen, PhD in Rural Economics, Iowa State University.

"Let's tune up the Winnebago, Mike," declared Krag. "And we'd better tune up our dueling points about our hope for change."

Chapter 7: Fox in the Hen-House

"Our radio audience sure is getting restless," reported Jim, with glee. "They're eager to hear about the time and place of encounter. And they wonder if KRRL will broadcast the duel.

"No, but an intriguing idea," he continued. "Maybe the University station will record it, and we can play the confrontation later."

"Well, we plan to announce the time and place in today's program," said Krag. "End of May. Got confirmation from the office of Professor Arnesen. Gather that he's eager for the showdown. Expects to horsewhip us. All to benefit rural economics, of course."

About noon, the phone rang. "Harry here. Just want to alert you. Seems we have a spy in town. Attractive young woman asked about you. Wouldn't give her name, but when I saw the University marking on the car in front of the store, I mentioned it. So she admitted she's from the Rural Economics Department. Scouting the community, she said. Spy, I'd say. Wants to talk with you, so she's on her way to track you down."

"Okay. Thanks. And I believe she just arrived. I'll report later," said Krag as he hung up the phone.

Krag whistled to himself in admiration when he watched the spy emerge from the car in front of the shop. He assumed she came to gather info for the debate.

"Yup, you guessed it," said the tall blonde, wearing jeans and a sweater that emphasized her attractive figure. "I'm a spy from our Rural Economics Department. Can't give you my name, of course, so I suppose you can just call me Agent X. The professor wants to know more about your community and your hopes for it."

"First, we can talk after I rustle up some grub," said Krag, "if you'll pardon my cowboy talk."

"Depends on the food," said X.

"Let me check with Annicka, my Danish cook," said Krag, as he headed for the house.

"Beef stew with chili, baking powder biscuits and rhubarb pie," he announced.

"Sounds delicious!" declared X. "And I'm hungry after hiking all around Grund, as you locals seem to call your place. Strange name for the distinguished Bishop Grundtvig, I'd say."

During lunch, Krag explained his hope for a regional center for a variety of purposes and services. He also told about his own attachment to his *Homestead*. On a tour of his grandparents' house, he showed the framed U.S. Homestead document.

"We heard in our department about your investing a lot of your considerable wealth in your *Homestead*," said X. "Also learned about the tragedy of your wife and children. So very sorry.

"Well, pard," she announced, "I think I should mosey on toward Ames. Make my report. By the way, as you probably realize, our University recognizes the significance of your ideas and supports them. The real purpose of the debate next week will be to promote healthy change for our area. And the publicity is generating positive support. The rate of change can't be predicted, but conditions for farms will be conspicuously different 25 years from now — 50 years, who will even remember present farming."

As X opened the car door, Harry came with Mike and Steve in tow.

"The other three of our team," said Krag, as he introduced them.

As she shook hands all around, she declared that she felt she could report back to the University with adequate information for the debate. "We expect, of course, a friendly encounter aimed at mutual benefit. The idea of a debate gets good attention to your radio program, though. See y'all next week. Lunch on us!"

"Speaking of food," said Mike, "maybe you could suggest some homemaking ideas we could share on the radio. Get more women interested. Women may not be interested in the kind of change we're talking about. But your ag school should be able to promote good grub."

As X rolled toward the highway, irritated about "good grub from the ag school," Harry gave a "thumbs up," not sensing the anger of an aggravated agent.

"Seems a lot friendlier than the professor. Quite savvy. And mighty good looking. Bet she knows Iowa tastes in food too."

"Yeah, and no rings," said Mike. "As we say in Iowa, you should cultivate that field, Krag."

"Count on us to back you up," added Steve. "We'll provide personal testimonies about your sterling character! And the sterling of your money! 'Land baron' to boot!"

"A winning hand, I'd say," concluded Steve. "A matched pair. Tall and slim. You about six-three, she nearly six. Both blond, blue eyes. Close in age, I'd guess. Both self-assured—well, maybe that's not so good."

"Hold on!" said Krag, raising his hands to indicate stop. "I had a great marriage and family, and I cherish that. Now I have my *Homestead* to work on, and I'm focused on the potential of our community to have significant regional impact."

"Well and good," responded Steve. "But we think you have too much to offer to stay in a shell of your past. At least Agent X, for instance, might prove interesting. And not limit you to local socializing."

"You agree to that too?" asked Krag, as he looked to Mike and Harry.

"Yup," from Mike, and "Me too," from Harry.

"Could help you balance your life," continued Steve, as the other two nodded agreement.

"Well," responded Krag, "thanks for your concern...and your conniving counsel.

"I do have to admit that X was interesting to talk with. Had a sense of spunk, too."

"Anyway, we want to challenge the Ivory Tower. So let's get down to brass tacks and point Winnie toward Ames.

"We can announce our intent and suggest a time during our next broadcast."

"Sounds okay to me," said Harry, suppressing a laugh. "Hope it's okay to Kay."

"If not," suggested Mike, "we'll just have to settle for our campaign to lasso Agent X. She seems like an interesting maverick."

Chapter 8: Airing Their Beliefs

"You guys are really going to do it?" chuckled Jim in the meeting with him at KRRL. "Take on the educational establishment. Might be slaughter—of you guys—but could be fun. And I love what it will do to our ratings."

"You sure your signal will reach as far as Ames?" inquired Steve.

"Flat as a pancake between here and there," Jim assured the quartet. "Well, perhaps a lumpy pancake. Obviously, they heard your broadcast before, and you goaded the academics enough to react. Now you promised to throw down the gauntlet. Let the games begin!"

Later, on air, Krag announced: "Well folks, this is Krag Jensen again, with my three henchmen. In this program, we are officially announcing our intent to invade Iowa State University at Ames.

"We have been challenged to a respectful debate about our belief that change is coming to our area, to our way of life, whether we like it or not.

"The head of the Department of Rural Economics at Iowa State has cautioned us—to put it bluntly, 'To hold our horses.'

"In the spirit of academia, we did elegantly call that advice to be horse manure. So we're heading that way to see if our ideas of change smell the way the professors say.

"Now I'll call on my three wranglers to add their two cents' worth. Maybe the word 'cents' should be spelled 'scents' to fit how we rustics have been addressed."

"I've been in business for a long time in the town of Grund," said Harry, "and I've seen the writing on the wall all along. As we heard in that play from up in Mason City, we've got trouble right here in Grund. Yes sir, we've got trouble!"

"What Harry means," said Mike, "is that the machinery, so to speak, of our little world in Iowa is wearing out. And that's not something I can fix in my garage. We have to adjust and improve the workings of our community in a variety of ways."

"We do hope the Rural Economics Department can help us see into the future," Steve added. "We were assured by a visitor from there that they too recognize the challenge of change—the kind of change that's showing itself on our horizon."

"Guess we don't need to say more in this broadcast," Krag concluded. "We will await the responses from Ames."

Once again, the quartet got the response right from the post office, when Jim showed the latest post card to Krag. In the usual telegraphic style, the card said "You're on." It confirmed the timing. Promised room and board in guest quarters on campus. Said a campus map is in the mail. "May the people of Iowa win!" Kay Anderson, PhD, Department of Rural Economics, Iowa State University.

A few days later, much of the town turned out to surround the Winnebago as the quartet prepared to head for battle.

"Our carriage is tuned up," said Mike.

"And well supplied with sandwiches, coffee and desserts," announced Krag.

"Start the engine," shouted Steve, as most of the crowd cheered—and drowned out the scattering of boo's.

Iowa State University
in Ames

Right on schedule, before noon, they parked the Winnebago as instructed by notes on the campus map. Off they went, decked out in their matching jeans, shirts, jackets and work boots, with a Fordson tractor imprinted on the shirt as a symbol of the past.

After they entered the building that housed the Department of Rural Economics, they marched down the long hallway toward the last office. Heads popped out as they went past other offices, some with grins, other just staring.

"Well, here we go, to our long-awaited encounter," announced Krag, at the door with the sign Prof. Kay Arnesen, Director of the Department of Rural Economics.

Inside, the receptionist smiled warmly and greeted them: "Welcome, we've been expecting you, of course. And right on time, too. Let me take you into the office of Dr. Arnesen."

While Krag thought of declaring, "Dr. Arnesen, I presume," he stopped in his tracks, staring into the face of Agent X. She smiled, reached out to shake hands.

"Agent X!" Krag blurted out.

"I'm also known as Dr. Arnesen—and welcome! I look forward to continuing our discussion. Sorry I had to spy on my adversaries to see if you were for real. I did find you to be informed and interesting. And hospitable.

"Now we want to return the favor. We'll join others from our faculty and staff for a lunchtime discussion."

Steve was the first to gather his wits, but even then he only mumbled, "I thought you were a man."

As Mike and Harry laughed, Harry declared simply: "No, definitely not a man."

"Hey Krag, did the cat get your tongue?" whispered Steve.

"Just flabbergasted by X," mumbled Krag.

Chapter 9: Analysis of Change

"Welcome to Dr. Arnesen's Round Table," came the greeting from Dr. Philip Stroud as Krag and trio plus Agent X entered the small dining room in the "faculty retreat center."

Dr. Kay then handled the remainder of the introductions, first of the visitors, and then the other "rural economists."

Noting the tenseness of the visitors, Dr. Phil assured them that they were among friends. "All of us here struggle with the imprecise challenge of looking ahead. Perhaps all of you have just felt comfortable with conditions as they are—when an apparently slight shift throws you for a loop."

"I know," said Mike, as he began to feel at ease with the elite group. "In my car-repair business, one modification after another left me high and dry until I finally got a handle on each one."

"Statistics drive me up the wall," said another professor. "Just when we think we've got a good interpretation of our numbers, a new figure pops up out of nowhere. At least we thought it came out of nowhere until we saw how it fit so naturally in our existing pattern. Unnerving all the same—makes us skittish about what will surprise us next."

"I'll underscore that reaction," interjected another member of the "round table." He explained that in his role as a psychologist, "I'm challenged to help others adapt to the latest surprises while at the same time developing a sense of anticipation about what might be just around the corner. And what might be the scope of that possibility."

"Well," commented Dr. Kay to Krag…and Harry, Mike and Steve…"this gives you an idea of the variables we cope with as we look ahead. And we haven't even alluded to the obvious changeable nature of nature—besides the many facets of human nature."

"Now that we've introduced you to our food for thought in our research and reactions," continued Dr. Kay, "why don't we check out our lunch layout. Serve yourself…and help yourself. We have the salad bar, the grill, breads, cold cuts, the dessert table, and coffee and other beverages. All from Iowa, of course. With a few exceptions," she acknowledged, with a smile.

Like the food choices, the continuing discussion included a widening range of ideas and issues related directly and indirectly to farmland economics of Iowa. The people involved, the impact of organizations and companies, the changing markets, and the growing scope of competition.

Dr. Kay then directed the discussion to the interests of the folks from Grundtvig. She asked Krag to tell about the history of his *Homestead* and about his hopes for it. Then the other three also joined in to tell of their shared hopes for a changing and expanding role of their community.

They acknowledged that even the ideas for change they offered in their radio commentary had caused concern from nearby small towns and schools.

"And I suspect we ain't seen nothin' yet," said Mike.

"In an even bigger way," added Krag, "I see related change in industry. Collins Radio, for example, started in Iowa, but now it has grown way beyond its early local base and its earlier products. More and more, I picture electronics and related applications moving west. Computers on the horizon there too. Like another gold rush."

Then Steve spoke up about the closure of the school shop where he had been the teacher. "To compete, we need to develop and refine skills related to electronics and product development, instead of closing shop."

"Even in agriculture," interjected Dr. Kay, "we see major competition erupting in the West, particularly California. We can't grow all they can, but perhaps our bread and butter products complement their specialties to serve a changing palate in America...and other parts of the world."

"We thank you all for the valuable sharing, but I think we've taken enough of your time," said Krag as he sensed the ticking of the clock. "I'm sure I can speak for our troupe that we've enjoyed and benefited from being part of your 'round table.' We hope you will continue to save a place for us in your research and projections about rural Iowa."

"Count on it," said Dr. Kay as she led a round of applause for the guests and rose to shake hands with them.

As Krag said 'so long' to her, he added quietly, "I enjoyed meeting you as Agent X and now humbly knowing you as Dr. Kay."

She smiled, and blushed slightly. "We'll keep an eye on your changing community.

"Now, Dr. Phil has offered our guests a tour of part of our campus—starting dramatically at the gallery of paintings by our noted Iowa artist, Grant Wood.

Iowa Cornfield
by Grant Wood

"By the way," she added, with a slight smile, "you'll see in some of the paintings that we do conduct research related to nutrition, such as flour.

"Maybe you can come for breakfast another time, and try our corn syrup on pancakes. And taste our cold cereal, which was one product we developed to simplify the cooking challenges for women. And the chemistry department has helped us come up with vegetable oils to make women's chores easier, such as polishing furniture and floors."

"Touché," declared Mike, with outreached hands in apology. "I made the mistake of belittling women when Dr. Kay visited us. Another lesson learned for me."

During the tour, Steve talked quietly with Dr. Phil. "Harry, Mike and I have noted that Dr. Kay and Krag seem compatible. He's a saddened widower, but we'd like to see him reconnect more with society. She seems suited to him, but we don't know her situation. Or interests."

"First, you don't need to use 'Dr.' with me, just Phil. As to Kay, she's unattached, but with a bitter memory about a professor who took advantage of her as a graduate assistant. Then that Romeo left her for another assistant. Fortunately, her concentration on education helped her recover. Since then, her career has dominated her life.

"I too detected a spark of hope for a growing friendship between her and Krag. She seemed to respond to his banter in a spirited manner, not in her more-typical no-nonsense way. So consider me Cupid's helper for encouraging that good feeling," smiled Phil.

Chapter 10: Review & Restart

Dr. Kay called for a quick huddle after the visitors left.

"A lark for our visitors or a spark for change?" she wondered.

"I applaud their concern about the need for change to ensure the health of rural Iowa…and all of the Midwest, for that matter," said Dr. Phil. "The wartime surge of our regional economy has leveled off. In various ways, the war diverted young men and women from life on the farm. As we know from experience right on the campus here, veterans have been capitalizing on government-sponsored education opportunities. And after such major disruption, you can't put the genie back in the barn, so to speak."

In a variety of expressions, the others of the department leadership echoed that assessment.

The professor of rural psychology endorsed the surprisingly sensible understanding from the visitors of the need for change. "From their small local outpost, they could be a viable seed for renewal."

"We could lend support by creating a task force to meet periodically to explore the concern," said Dr. Kay. "Our institution would be represented, of course, plus farm organizations, various parts of government, agriculture publishers and other media as well as appropriate industries.

"Maybe even former Vice President Henry Wallace. He was also a past Secretary of Agriculture. Noted publisher. And he is an alum. Available? And desirable? Hard to say."

"Whatever, a good first step," said Dr. Phil, "and I nominate you, Dr. Kay, to lead the way. Certainly Krag Jensen could speak for rural communities."

"A task force seems logical," she responded. "Not likely to involve a lot of time, effort and money. Could generate considerable attention—mostly positive, I'd expect. And serve to explore and respond to concerns.

"I agree, it would make sense to seek participation by Krag Jensen. He brought this to our attention, and he seems to have the stature and dedication to advocate for rural change."

Meanwhile, in the Winnebago on the way back to Grundtvig, the discussion followed a parallel path. The quartet agreed that the meeting at the University proved to be productive.

"Seems like we have a University on our side," said Steve.

"Now we can change the tone of our broadcasts toward harmony and advocacy rather than confrontation," said Krag. "For now we can at least allude to support from the University until we get further confirmation from Dr. Arnesen."

"Speaking of Dr. Arnesen," smiled Steve, "she sure turned out to be a surprise—and a pleasant one."

"And a beauty," added Mike, with a wolf whistle for emphasis.

"Proved to be friendly and helpful, once we broke the ice," said Harry. "Hope we see more of her."

"Me too," agreed Krag, with a smile about the obvious romantic encouragement.

"Well, I did some snooping on your behalf, Krag," said Steve. "I confirmed that she is single and unattached. Still not fully recovered from a past betrayal, though.

"So I think we should move slowly and steadily to get on her good side," he added.

"Yeah, she's probably a bit skittish," stated Mike. "We hafta be patient."

"Maybe we need to conduct more of a background check," said Harry. "Don't want to appear too eager at a time she might be wary."

"Hey," Krag interrupted, "to quote from an earlier message from her, 'Hold your horses!' Who says I want you guys to pursue her for me?"

"Well, we voted on it," said Mike.

"For your own good," added Harry.

"And we like her," Steve said, with a 'thumbs up.'

"Then we should change the tone of our broadcasts to indicate your interest and good intentions," Harry stated. "We can admit that our talk about a duel was just an exaggerated form of humor to get listener attention. Should help make sure we welcome her participation."

"Okay," Krag declared, "if you guys can set aside romance, let's plan our new friendlier broadcasts. We do want to convey the cooperation we sensed in our visit to Iowa State University. And express our gratitude."

At KRRL, Jim was all ears as he listened to their report. He indicated lack of surprise to learn of the cooperative response from the University.

Before Jim could ask, Krag reported that the mysterious Agent X turned out to be Dr. Kay Arnesen, head of the Department of Rural Economics at the University.

"What a surprise!" added Mike. "A real dish! Well, more of a handsome sophisticated babe in her conservative business suit.

"I believe she impressed Krag too," he continued, with a wink toward Jim. "We hope that has potential. A pair to draw to!"

"These guys have become conspiring Cupids," countered Krag. "Born promoters. Of course, that's why I'm glad to have them promoting our cause about the future of Iowa."

After Jim welcomed his "roving quartet" back from their junket to Iowa State University, Krag told of the helpful and encouraging support they received when they visited there.

"Your momentum grows," said Jim. "Cards and letters and phone calls keep coming in. Only a few 'worry warts' concerned that rural life as we have known it will change. Once again, we'll tally them for your possible response on air."

"Our next program will emphasize the cooperation we found at the University," Krag explained. "We'll downplay the duel as just some verbal horseplay and tell about the helpful information we received. Our new friends at the University acknowledged that their research often seems like a bowl of Jell-O as it shifts around with the latest input. But they're detecting some important economic and social trends."

"Take it from me also," said Steve. "They see trends that we have only been guessing at. They can pin down patterns that confirm what we've been harping about on this program—life in our future is not going to be the same as in the past."

From that opening, the four shared thoughts, ideas and concerns. And they stressed their hope that change will be positive, for the over-all good of the people of Iowa.

After the program, Krag invited Jim to swing by the *Homestead* on Saturday night. "I plan to host a shindig to celebrate our successful testing of our ideas, and KRRL has been an import part of our pitch.

"The others are already in on it, and this will offer a good chance for all of us to get better acquainted. Especially the families, yours included, who have been left on the sidelines, puzzled about what we have been up to."

"Thanks for that," said Jim. "I look forward to it, and so will my wife and kids. And I thank you again for getting all the positive attention to KRRL. Your word is spreading, and so is our reach in the area."

Krag also realized he was overdue in personally thanking the folks at the University. His call connected directly with Dr.

Kay. "Agent X—how good to talk with you again. I guess you can tell by my greeting who this is."

"Sure can," she replied, "with your enthusiastic tone. Hope you and your colleagues benefited from your time here."

"Indeed we did," said Krag, "and I felt I should let you know our appreciation. And I have a couple of other thoughts to share with you as well."

"Okay, shoot."

"First, I'm planning a shindig here in two weeks at my *Homestead* and am inviting my three colleagues and families to help celebrate the restoration of my grandparents' house. Jim Stardad of our radio station KRRL and his family will join us, as will the contractor, crew and families. Thought it might be an opportunity for you and your associates to rub shoulders with us common folks. Sorry about the short notice, but think it over and let me know."

"Congratulations on the restoration," Dr. Kay responded. "I got a glimpse of your mansion when I visited you. And I'd certainly like a tour. The gathering sounds interesting—and fitting for our informal research about Iowa. Let me check with the others and get back to you.

"Now," she added, "for question number two."

"I understand that your University includes a section for Architecture/Engineering, and I might need that kind of help in repurposing my horse barn. Long time since it was used

that way, and I don't expect to stock work horses—or riding horses. But I think the handsome barn that Grandfather designed could become my office and garage. Sort of a metaphor for changing times in Iowa."

"Hmmm," Dr. Kay responded, "I'm trying to imagine that."

"Picture this," explained Krag. "I see the possibility of a prefabricated structure installed inside the barn, with my office on top of a garage. Heated and air conditioned, of course. Make use of a bunch of my thermal switches in the controls, naturally," Krag added, with his typical chuckle.

"You've certainly piqued my curiosity," admitted Dr. Kay. "It will be a treat to spring that on my friend, who heads Architecture/Engineering.

"I'm sure you can count on us to drop by to explore that challenge," she added. "So I'll let you know about both of your invitations."

A week later, she called: "I hope our RSVP isn't too late. We, would include Dr. Phil and his wife and me. And Dr. Frank Carlson of Architecture/Engineering would like to join us for a sneak peak at the barn you want to convert. And his wife would like to accompany us as well."

"Great news!" Krag responded. "Visitors from the University will make a big splash at our gathering. And I hope you will accept me as your consort."

"Consort. That sounds…intriguing," answered Dr. Kay.

"Fits me. I'm unattached," said Krag, "except for slowly fading grief for my family."

"And I'm unattached," offered Dr. Kay, "now that I've pushed an unfortunate association out of my memory.

"Guess I'll take my chances and say 'yes.' After all, you are the master of the manor."

"Make that *Homestead*," corrected Krag, as Dr. Kay laughed softly.

"Super! I'll send a map, details about the time and a list of players," continued Krag. "Casual attire, of course, like a picnic."

"Alas," stated Dr. Kay, "we don't have a Winnebago, so we'll just have to squeeze into the department sedan. You know, the same one as before, when I visited as Agent X. Can't miss it. Look for the University logo on the door."

"It, and you, will be a welcome sight. See you then," concluded Krag as he hung up the receiver. With a smile on his face.

Chapter 11: Roadrunners & Winnie

As Jim and the quartet examined the batch of phone messages and cards and letters that had accumulated at KRRL, they were surprised to see invitations requesting them to speak at schools and communities.

"Looks like we'll have to join that Toastmasters organization," laughed Mike. "I've heard of them anyway, but not here."

"Guess we'll have to start our own speechifying organization," announced Harry, "so we can develop a solid and interesting message to share. And defend."

"We've sorta been doing that already," Steve reminded them, "for our broadcasts, in our discussions, and our reviews of what we said. Not to mention the blunt critiques from our own families."

"Maybe we should test the water right here at home," said Krag. "The local business folks and other leaders want us to appear at one of their meetings. We can learn from their reactions. Sink or swim among friends. Maybe they would rescue us if we flounder. Could help prepare us before we go on the road with our show."

"Guess I can help as a kind of booking agent for you guys," said Jim. "You are doing a lot to boost my business."

"Thanks for the offer," said Krag. "You know the territory, what reactions we might expect, and how we should plan a schedule. After all, some of my teammates have to work for a living, even if I don't. But more and more, my *Homestead* is my job."

"Okay," Jim acknowledged, "time to start the 'rubber chicken' circuit. Our local folks meet for lunch at the diner. They'll provide you free lunch, and allow about half an hour for a presentation, plus a few more minutes to answer questions."

"You set the time, and we'll try to get our ideas and assignments organized," agreed Krag.

"For our 'dog & pony show,' I think we should have a set of large cards to emphasize our main points," added Steve. "Once we boil down our key words, I can have Hank prepare them at his print shop. He can letter them to be bold enough to be visible from the back of a large room. Then we can select and organize the cards to fit a specific situation."

The night before their inaugural presentation, they made a dry run, practicing their parts and arranging their oversized cards to emphasize key points.

At noon the next day, the "interlocutor" introduced them and welcomed them as friends. After nervously eating their "rubber chicken," they launched into their theme about dealing with and causing change.

Following applause, the meeting leader thanked them for the clear and strong presentation. Then they fielded several questions by acknowledging challenges and offering specific suggestions related to coping with and capitalizing on change.

Then, at the conclusion, the school superintendent asked if they would present a similar message in a forum hosted by the school. "No rubber chicken, though," he laughed…with guffaws from others.

Later, while looking back and ahead, the quartet, plus Jim, noted particular support for and concern about their pitch. Harry and Mike reminded the others that in their businesses they hear reactions from others in the community. Mostly enthusiasm about potential for the future, but a degree of worry about the changing nature of competition, like the earlier impact of the mail-order companies such as Sears and Wards.

"For now," Krag suggested, "we can simply call attention to the school forum during our next broadcast, pointing to the challenges of educating for the future. And we can emphasize the need for ongoing education for all people in many forms. Even on radio, with programs prepared for learning."

"I definitely vote for that," laughed Jim. "I do think radio offers an underutilized tool for education, and we have access to lots of resources and skilled presenters."

"We could develop and make available a range of printed material to support the teaching," Steve indicated. "Colleges, government agencies such as the extension programs, including the 4H Clubs and FFA. Good chance many companies would recognize an opportunity to share. And publishers as well as the broadcast media might want to get in on it."

"Don't forget the ethnic groups in the area, with our town of Grundtvig at the center of the Danish concentration," added

Harry. "Already we Danes push hard at learning, not only our culture, but the importance of adapting to all kinds of growth—just like our ancestors did after they arrived as immigrants. They didn't get in a rut, nor should we!"

"I'm certainly with you," Krag declared, "because my Danish roots grew right in this community. And my Grandfather Jensen loved new ideas and how to put them in practice."

"That characteristic certainly has shown in you, Krag," Steve stated. "Seems to me that you've been on the leading edge of change all your life. And we count on a lot more to come!"

Little did the quartet expect the large turnout for the forum about change, with focus on the role of education. As they scanned the full house in the gymnasium, Jim chuckled as he reminded them of the power of promotion. KRRL especially, he alluded to, but also the coverage in the local weekly newspaper. And an expanding radius of outreach.

After the superintendent introduced them, they got a loud welcome of applause, led by the community leaders who knew them. Then they launched into their exploration of change, with emphasis on the critical role of education in its widest application. They outlined the many methods for learning—well beyond the three-R's type of rote study at many schools.

They shared insights they had gained from the Department of Rural Economics at Iowa State University. Using data gathered and provided by that department, they showed the importance of learning suited to changes in agriculture, industry, commerce, medicine, professions, trades and

politics. They emphasized that in most cases, changes through cooperation and consolidation served the common good.

"Not unlike the lessons learned and applied by the Founding Fathers of our nation," Krag noted. "They struggled to advance from a weak assortment of Colonies to a strong Union of States. Not without a lot of give and take and trial and error, which we in Iowa and much of the Midwest in particular will have to cope with to achieve progress."

After vigorous applause, the audience participation opened with several friendly expressions of thanks and approval. Then the tone of the gathering shifted, as one after another of the worriers spoke up.

Shouted one grumbler: "Who appointed you to become the conscience of our communities, promoting change that we haven't asked for or want?"

Threshing

"Blame me for our self-appointed committee," said Krag. "I came home, so to speak, to my grandfather's farm, where I had spent several summers as a kid. This time I came with scientific, commercial, financial and industrial knowledge and experience. From my perspective, I saw a revolution in agricultural methods and products. And changes in land ownership. And I saw the exodus of a slew of Midwesterners heading for the aircraft and other industries of the West Coast. So I sensed the need to understand change all around us here in Iowa."

Then another dissident interrupted: "You come here from Chicago and preach to us about unifying around a town like Grund. What will that do to our small towns, our schools, our churches—everything our communities have provided?"

"Let me have a whack at that," Steve shouted over the grumbling of several in the audience. "Maybe your communities can be the spokes in a wheel, important as they revolve around a strong hub. Your schools, stores and services could benefit from support from the center, including a share in the tax revenue of the wheel. Improving communication systems could help you stay connected—but still stay independent in many ways."

After Steve's "oratory," the superintendent called for a close of the meeting. "After all," he said, "tomorrow's a school day."

A week later, a phone call interrupted Krag's reverie about the nature of change.

"Hi, this is Agent X."

"Great!" answered Krag. "I love to hear from my No. 1 spy. What have you gleaned now?"

"Well," Dr. Kay answered, "our department has been sharing the story from your newspaper. *The Sower*—I like that name. Sounds as though you had good give and take at your town meeting. Maybe a split decision, but in your favor. Congratulations on a rousing start for campaign about change!"

"All our success we owe to you," chuckled Krag, "because we invoked the University when we needed to show some muscle."

"Not the way we read it," Dr. Kay countered. "Sounds as though you guys offered a convincing philosophical and practical picture of the future. And the need to adapt. Keep it up. We in Iowa need more of that."

"Thanks much!" responded Krag. "Your interest and comments mean a lot to me!

"Hope you got all information about our *Homestead* picnic. I look forward to serving as the personal tour guide to a consort. "

"I look forward to my role as a consort—whatever that implies in your town. I suspect your local newspaper just might be the sower of gossip about a consort."

"No doubt—after I provide some newsworthy comments," chuckled Krag.

"With that to wonder about," said Dr. Kay, "I think I will just hang up—and hope for the best, but prepare for the worst. See you soon!"

Chapter 12: Housewarming Party

To arrange for the *Homestead* picnic, Krag suggested to his cook Annicka that she enlist the help of the women at the Danish Lutheran Church.

"Umm!" exclaimed Krag. "I've tasted their food and know I can count on gourmet grub."

"You know at the church we simply prepare American dishes, sometimes with a Danish touch," cautioned Annicka. "Well, we can offer our delicious *aebleskiver* as a special treat. After we serve our Iowa fare of meat and potatoes. And homemade bread and jam. Rhubarb pie of course. Lemonade, lots of coffee."

"Smells like good home-cooking," declared Krag. "Mouthwatering to think about! Perfect for our visitors from our agricultural university, too."

"Then I guess I'd better recruit the top team from the church," said Annicka. "Put our best food forward," she added, with a shy smile about her pun.

"Whoa," laughed Krag. "A cook cooking up jokes too!"

By the day of the 'housewarming picnic', Annicka had her troupe in action, preparing the meal and waiting to serve.

When the University sedan pulled into the yard of the *Homestead*, the first reaction of the visitors was "Umumm good!" as they smelled the tantalizing home-cooking.

Krag came to the car to greet them: "Smells great, doesn't it!"

As he shook hands with Dr. Kay, they smiled at each other as she declared that "I sense Iowa in that delicious smell. Maybe with a hint of Denmark."

Then Dr. Phil stepped forward to shake hands and introduce his wife Janet. Next he directed Krag to Dr. Carlson and his wife Thora.

"Welcome to the Jensen *Homestead*," declared Krag, as he beckoned his three cohorts forward to greet the five from the University.

After that, he waved for Annicka, declaring the guests should meet the source of the welcoming smell of food. "She serves me almost every day of the week…and Sunday too at our church. Sometimes even her grandchildren help—at least by waiting tables. And they helped set up our temporary picnic tables and benches, thanks to a loan of materials from Harry's lumber yard."

Annicka blushed at the attention, while she shook hands with the visitors.

As she hustled back to her food preparation, Dr. Kay mentioned that during the drive down to Grundtvig the University car was filled with conversation about the Jensen *Homestead*. And your crusade about change.

"We'll be curious about the presentations you mentioned on the phone. In particular the gathering at the school," said Dr. Kay.

"Well," chuckled Krag, "as a noted spy, you probably got wind of the reactions. Quiet compliments and loud complaints, such as the threats to a way of life in the

communities, schools, churches. Even to the traditional ways of farming."

"Not surprising," Dr. Phil interjected, with a restrained grin. "Even at our University, change faces challenge, often related to shifts in some of the simplest procedures. From us, who are supposed to be advocates of advancement."

"I recently learned that the history of Iowa higher education includes a link with a famous — or notorious — person exposing a changing world," said Krag.

"How's that?" asked Dr. Phil.

"Wasn't there a Veblen teaching in Iowa many years ago?" continued Krag.

"Oh, you mean Andrew Veblen, who taught at Luther College in Decorah and the University of Iowa. And his son Oswald Veblen graduated from the University of Iowa and went on to fame in geometry," replied Dr. Phil.

"Andrew's more famous brother, Thorstein Veblen, taught many places, but not in Iowa. But yes, Thorstein Veblen certainly analyzed and exposed change as he explored the connection between economics and sociology. Should be interesting to discuss with you about Thorstein's thoughts regarding the 'leisure class'--which you and the rest of us here might well be part of.

"With his weird womanizing, he might not, however, be the best topic to explore among the Iowa folks you want to influence," Dr. Phil concluded.

"Good reminder," said Krag, "about communication that fits our situation. But I'd certainly be interested in learning more about the Veblens at another time."

"Here's something you can sink your teeth into right now," interjected Thora. "One *Homestead* modification you shared with Kay certainly generated excitement on our way down," added Thora. "Frank speculated every which way about how you might convert your barn into an office. We also talked about the old-fashioned red grain elevator we saw at the edge of town—in contrast to the huge and shiny storage cylinders that seem to prevail now."

"I have my dibs on that old grain elevator now that it's nearly abandoned," Krag responded. "Plan to move it out here. Of course, I could use some engineering advice for the move and how we might use it here. Just a hint in case you might have some advice, Frank. Don't need an answer right now though," chuckled Krag.

"I'll take it under advisement," said a cautious Frank. "But your matching barns really caught our attention, especially the graceful curved shape of the roofs. What's the story there?"

"My Grandfather Jensen seemed to have an intuitive sense of shape and symmetry," explained Krag. "He had some actual involvement in construction before that, and he studied as

much as he could. Even as a kid, I served as a sounding board for some of his ideas. Maybe that process started me toward my own form of design in electronics."

"All the more enticing to think about," Frank said, "and I look forward to a personal tour, especially of that horse barn that you want to convert to a new life."

"Coming up, after our picnic. First, I think you'll appreciate the mixed décor inside the house. Items from my grandparents and what I added later," announced Krag.

"I'm for that," exclaimed Janet. "Sounds intriguing, to see and hear about your *Homestead* renewal, Krag."

The animated discussion continued during and after the picnic meal— about the food, the setting, the history of the Homestead Act and its Iowa impact, and specifically the *Homestead* started by Krag's great-grandfather.

The review of history continued as the visitors from the community and the University discussed the restored house, with its original design influenced by Krag's great-grandmother as well his great-grandfather.

"Maybe the early electrical system here influenced my choice of career," Krag explained, "because Grandfather liked to tell about the generator and batteries and the wiring and fixtures and lights and outlets. Naturally, he regaled about Edison, and he pointed out that Ben Franklin discovered the concept of the lightning rods on all the buildings.

"Now, thanks to the construction crew," added Krag, "we've updated and expanded the system. We have a central hub for the new power input from the county. Even includes a generator for backup. Underground wiring fans out to the house, the horse barn and the granary.

"Kay, you'll be intrigued by that granary," added Krag. "It includes a network of bins and chutes to store and distribute various grains—that might turn into special flour mixes. The crib along the alley of the granary can store and dry corn and similar products. Just awaiting research help from the University."

"What about that other large, rambling buildings beyond the horse barn?" asked Frank.

"I don't hold fond memories of the cattle and pigs housed there—except for the friendly kittens. Otherwise, just sweat and stink! Grandfather just let those grow like Topsy, without a good design," explained Krag.

"But now our radio team does have a wish—for a retail complex," continued Krag. "Those structures crowd the edge of town and butt along the new Interstate. Could include a service station, restaurant and stores. And, in the practicality of centuries of co-operative endeavors in Denmark, we could involve the community of Grundtvig as investors, customers and workers."

"Watch out," cautioned Frank, "that might continue to grow like Topsy."

"Well, that's where we'd like your help," said Steve. "To achieve our goal, we would need a plan—and consultants and contractors—to convert that spread into a useful purpose. And to create a financial structure as well."

"Oh, I can see it now!" exclaimed Phil. "This would serve as a valuable case study for our Department of Rural Economics in our ongoing assessment of co-ops of past and present. And how co-ops might impact the future."

Chapter 13: Barn-Raising Plan

As Krag led the visitors to the next stage of the tour, he announced: "We aren't horsing around now, Frank. The horses are gone from this barn, and we want to convert it for my personal use. Let's go to the top—to the place for my new office suite.

"So we'll head up this ladder to the haymow for an 'overview,' you might say," he explained, with a chuckle. "Follow me Kay, and I'll give you a hand, with the others right behind."

Krag continued to hold her hand as he led her toward an unusual feature of the haymow—a basketball hoop. As the others, including Krag's team, gathered around, he explained that his grandfather had installed that for him and the neighborhood kids. Grandfather even shot some baskets and joined in a scrimmage once in a while," chuckled Krag. "I finally caught up with him in height at six-three, but not then. Of course, being Grandfather, he used his height to advantage. Always capitalizing on opportunity."

"Aha," announced Kay, "we get some more insight into your character, Krag. Interesting revelation."

"Okay, Frank," said Krag, "I hope you see what I see."

"Oh yes, I think so," Frank answered. "Modern efficiency in maximized space. A simple but state-of-the-art box set in a traditional, handsome farm structure. Heating, air conditioning, lighting, electronics, plumbing. And if we add a tall enough antennae, television should be accessible—if desirable.

"Real downtown," laughed Frank, "but way ahead of downtown. In this charming rustic setting."

"What a combination!" exclaimed Kay, as all around her others agreed, with nods and smiles.

Back on the ground floor, Krag declared, "Naturally, my vehicles, including Grandfather's restored Fordson and Ford F8 tractors, need some tender loving care," said Krag as he removed the canvas covers from both.

"I learned to drive on that newer one—or not-so-old one," laughed Kay, "so I request that it gets reserved parking. And that I get to drive it when I come to visit again."

"They and my truck and special car will stay on the ground floor," added Krag, "with a certain amount of climate-control to keep them fit as a fiddle. Maybe heat under the driveway too…save on some snow shoveling."

Tucker

"Now I'm curious," said Kay. "What is that special car you alluded to? Something else I might want to drive?"

"I do think you would," Krag responded, containing his enthusiasm as he unveiled a Tucker. "A '48 Tucker...guess that was the basic one."

"A Tucker!" came the response from the visitors, almost in unison.

"How did you snag that rare bird?" a still-astounded Phil inquired.

"I knew Preston Tucker in Chicago," explained an enthusiastic Krag. "Shared interests in electronics as well as cars, especially my thermal-control devices for cars. We also compared notes about legal challenges.

"Right now I just store it in a secure place. Probably not for driving, just to be hauled on a special trailer for exhibitions. It will sure get lots of attention and could be another symbol of change!" exclaimed Krag. "These days, most young people have never heard of it, but find it an interesting curiosity. A few old-timers can enlighten them.

"Sorry Kay. Maybe we can get it ready to run again... someday."

"I'd like a shot at revving it up!" grinned Mike. "The first models included parts salvaged from the junk yard. Kinda patched together from other cars. Guess we could try that too, as the last resort."

"You going to continue to store it here?" asked Frank.

"Hope to," responded Krag. "That would be another design challenge for you...protected space for the Tucker."

"Another interesting challenge!" declared Frank, with nodding support from the others.

"Sorry, dreamers, but it's time to head out in our humble University car," announced Kay.

"So, Frank," said Kay as she picked up again on the topic of the buildings, "there's another reason for the barn make-over—to preserve that Tucker.

"Do you think you and your department and assorted contractors can—and will want to—take this on?"

"Chance of a lifetime!" exclaimed Frank. "Wouldn't miss it!"

"Okay...then we're good to go," said Krag.

"What a dramatic statement you'll be making, Krag, about change," said Phil. "Preserving the past while looking to the future!"

"By the way," added Kay, "we hope to put together a task force with a variety of state leaders to get on the band-wagon of change. Of course, we'd want you on the task force to represent your area."

"I'm complimented," answered a surprised Krag. "Glad you want us represented."

"Just in the embryo stage right now," responded Kay, "so we'll keep you posted on the progress. And when and where we might meet."

"Well...thanks," said Krag. "Another good reason to see you again," he added, as he recovered from the surprise.

Later, as the visitors said their goodbyes on the way toward the car, they praised the food and gave thumbs-up to the tour and conversations.

As Krag started to open the car door for Kay, he paused: "Is it okay to hug a professor?"

Encouraged by a unanimous "yes," Krag wrapped his arms around Kay and declared: "Great to have the company of a lovely and charming consort."

"And I enjoyed the role," smiled Kay.

"Maybe," he added, "you'd be willing to repeat that when I call on the folks at Deere. Another pair of eyes, especially those of a spy, might by helpful in gathering information."

"Well," she hesitated, "it could be an important connection for our department. So let's plan on it."

"And you'll be hearing from our department," Frank assured Krag, "with at least a preliminary analysis of your barn raising."

"Once again," said Thora, "your barns with their curved rafters will leave a lasting and pleasing impression. Thanks for sharing that, your thoughts about your Tucker and today's picnic with us.

"Phil and I will have much to talk about," Janet added, "as we speculate about the form and scope of the changes in

society that lie ahead. I hope that you're able to do what you visualize, to help shape the future."

As the University car pulled away, Krag asked his teammates if they could huddle with him, after the dust has settled from the picnic.

"We can share some leftovers while we ponder some leftover thoughts from the day," he suggested.

"Both kinds of leftovers appeal to me," said Steve. "We heard some stimulating thoughts while savoring that good cooking, too. Maybe we can share some more of both."

"A thought to consider," Krag suggested, "is that our entire community might enjoy an open house like this. And we can expand and test out our 'dog and pony show' before we take it on the road. I think we can count on most of our own community to be on our side already--and willing to adapt to the change we've alluded to for our area, our state and beyond."

But a few days later, a postcard arrived to dampen Krag's optimism:

Heard about your barn-raising aim. Beware—your aims to reshape the world could backfire... and turn into a barn-razing!

When Krag and team gathered at KRRL to air their next program, they and Jim puzzled about the postcard.

"Mailed from Des Moines," noted Jim, "Local enough to learn what's happening here in Grund."

"Barn-razing indicates fire," commented Harry. "Sounds scary, and could be a threat to all of us."

"Unfortunately," interjected Krag, "the protective sprinkler system I mentioned to our visitors will call for a long wait to become a reality. So we will just have to stay alert for anything suspicious."

Then Jim spoke up: "I frequently talk with the dispatchers at the state patrol about any warnings they would like to put on the air. This time I could warn them about the threat to us."

"Good idea," Mike affirmed. "I service some of their patrol cars, so I can mention our concern to their drivers."

"Guess we just have to sit tight for now," Steve concluded, "and wait and watch for any more messages, to see if this is just a prank."

"Hope the possibility of a prank proves to be the case," said Krag. "But we should try to track down the source so we can put our minds at rest."

During the next broadcast, they didn't share their concerns about the threats. They had agreed to down-play the message on the postcard with the hope it was just a lark by some jokester. But a week later, the Postmaster called them and Jim to come in to see and talk about the latest postcard.

The Postmaster reached dramatically for a postcard on his desk. When he held it up, they could see the charred edges. Came from Des Moines again. He commented that it didn't seem to be humor from high school kids.

He passed the card around, so all five could read the bizarre warning:

Your Socialism fries me! Could burn your butts too!

"Crude printing," Krag noted. "Crude language too. Maybe a foreigner. Or maybe faked."

"Some recent immigrants seem to be popping-up here and there," Harry mentioned, "but haven't heard of any trouble involving them."

"Time to update the state patrol," Jim suggested. "Maybe they can pass the information about the latest threats to a higher level. Even to the FBI."

"We should also let our local constables know what's happening," said Larry, "though I think they've already got wind of something cooking—so to speak. Don't want to shout fire at just a whiff of smoke. Still, an ounce of prevention could be important."

"I do think we must avoid commentary on our radio program," Krag added. "That would stir the embers too soon and too much. We can acknowledge that the nature of change affects different people in different ways. Some just 'go along to get along,' others remain wary but willing, and others stay worried and resistant.

"Guess we'll just have to try to reassure all of them that we favor progress, slow and steady, so we aren't left behind in a changing world. Heck, even the climate seems to be changing, so we have to keep an eye on that…and wonder why. And wonder what we can do about it—if anything." "Sorry to admit that cars and other gas guzzlers do have a negative effect on the air we breathe," Mike speculated. "Not like Los Angeles, but many towns in the Midwest burn coal to generate electricity. And that does add to the problem. But we should be able to mention that without stirring up a hornets' nest."

"Hey," interrupted Jim, "with the present tone, we sound a bit like the grim reaper—if you'll pardon the link to harvesting."

"Shocking!" laughed Steve. "Just let me groan about grain."

"Whoa," countered Harry, "as Jack Benny would say, 'Cut that out!' Just because we are on K-rural KRRL, we do have our standards."

"Anyway," laughed Jim, "you're doing what I intended to mention. We need some fun in the broadcast. Did you guys sing at school, and now at church? Let me answer that: I know you did and still do. So I think you should create a barbershop quartet. An Iowa tradition right out of *The Music Man*. And we can write lyrics to promote your cause. Another way to get your message across."

"Corny…but that's Iowa too," said Steve, in his bass tones. "I'm rusty, but willing. And it could be fun…for us anyway."

"I'll sing along with that," warbled Mike, a lot higher. "And, Krag and Larry, you can take up the middle. We did some singing to pass the time when we went in the Winnie to Ames. Sort of fit together."

"I'll direct," chuckled Jim, "and I'll enlist help from the new music teacher, who's working wonders with the high school kids. We can have a good time—even if not prime time. You guys can practice before our next broadcast. Even go on the air if your audition passes muster with the music teacher."

"Now I can understand how you succeed in selling advertising, Jim," Steve laughed. "You sure sucked us in on this gig, and we didn't even realize what hit us. 'Hit Parade' here we come!"

Two weeks later, as the foursome tuned up for their broadcast, worrying and wondering if they could actually sing on air, Jim came in with an attractive and assertive-looking woman in tow.

"Hey guys," announced Jim, "meet your new music director."

"Hi," she greeted with a strong alto tone, "I'm your new music dictator, Marla Madsen."

"Welcome," Krag said cautiously. "I guess we expected a man."

"Sorry to disappoint you…." she answered.

"Oh, I didn't mean that," said Krag, as he took in the tall and attractive director. "I guess you're Danish too," he added, not knowing how else to answer.

"Darn Danish is what some of the high school students evidently call me. Or something like that," she laughed. "And that means I darn well expect good results. With you guys too. Jim said that you've sung together for fun. So let's hear it. How about *Old MacDonald Had a Farm?*"

"Guess we can handle that," indicated Steve. "Might make an appropriate song for the program too."

She listened—grimaced, grinned, pondered. Put her hand to her ear to signal increased volume.

Then she offered her appraisal. "Jim said your short program might benefit from some fun. A little barbershop. From what I heard, I think we can do it. Not polished, but good enough will be good enough. And you'll get better, but why wait around. Try it. Maybe listeners will like it, we hope.

"Anyway, I got wind of your 'cause celebre'...."

"Huh?" asked Mike.

"I was referring to your crusade about acceptance of change, which sounds good to me. And Jim and I thought some fun music might make your serious message more palatable.

"So I've changed the words of *I'm Beginning To See The Light* to relate to Iowa, like this, as she sang with appealing gusto:

I never cared much for moonlit skies
I never wink back at fireflies
But now with new stars in Iowa skies,
I'm beginning to think otherwise.

"Got it?" she asked. "Then let's hear it!"

"Maybe you should sing for us," said Steve.

"No way!" said the Dictator Dane. "Good enough is good enough—for now," she said. "You'll be on the air. You'll get better. But my heavens!" she laughed. "Will you be our new stars?"

Response came quickly and positively, as Jim reported phone calls in favor of the new songbirds.

But then a call came from the state patrol to report a burning haystack near town. And a birthday candle on a nearby fence post. The kind of candle that won't blow out.

The mutual reaction: Stay in touch.

A week later, the Postmaster called them together again. "Almost missed this card," he said. "Stuck to other mail. Has spots of wax."

"Let's see what threat we get this time," said Krag, as he read the message:

Your song of light fired me up. Lit just one candle of protest. Enough to torch the haystack.

"Same crude letters...and drops of wax. Des Moines postmark again," continued Krag, as he passed the card around.

Then Jim saw Marla picking up her mail, so he invited her into the office.

"Good reactions to your barbershop quartet," Jim said to her, "but the burning of a nearby haystack appears to be a reaction too," as he showed her the postcard.

"What's he after?" asked Marla. "Oops! Guess I shouldn't assume the writer is a man," as she smiled at Krag.

"Not sure," said Krag. "Seems to protest the acceptance of the idea of change that we promote. Don't know of any personal link, unless the firebug has some personal grievance against one of us. No telling what that might be."

"Creepy," Steve admitted. "Can't predict, but could be a prelude to worse problems, including threats to people."

"The state patrol is on it," Jim reminded them. "Don't know who else might want to be involved."

The next morning, Krag's phone rang: "Hi, it's Kay. Heard about the fire. Radio news report referred to mysterious threats. Just had to call to be sure you folks are okay."

"Thanks for the call. Good to hear your warm and friendly voice. Yeah, we're okay, but the weird postcards we've received worry us."

"What kind of cards?" Kay wondered.

"The latest tied in with burning that haystack," Krag explained. "Even had drops of wax on it. Probably from the kind of birthday candle that doesn't go out when blown. Evidently that was the method used to start the fire in the haystack. The firebug left a similar candle near the haystack by putting it on top of a nearby fencepost."

"That is scary," exclaimed Kay. "Be careful! And keep us informed.

"And, by the way, we certainly enjoyed and learned from our visit to Grundtvig. Frank's exploring some ways to help you.

We are all still talking about the impact of the Veblen clan, especially the ideas of Thorstein. And we're intrigued by the Veblen family's connection to Iowa."

"Likewise," Krag responded. "An impressive example of an immigrant family changing with the times, especially capitalizing on education."

"With that, I'll say goodbye...and take care," said Kay.

"You too," said Krag. "Hope to talk with you again...soon!"

At the next broadcast, Jim announced "good news and bad news."

"Okay, how about the bad first," said Krag.

"Everybody in town and the surrounding area seems to be worried, based on the report from downtown and by phone calls and mail to the station. Interest from law enforcement folks grows daily too. But no clue—that they mentioned anyway, such as conspicuous tire tracks or footprints, even around the haystack. Police in Des Moines are on the lookout, as well."

"After that, the good news will be welcome," declared Harry. "Hope your millions of listeners liked our singing."

"Surprisingly, yes," Jim answered. "Oh, I should say—naturally. Called it 'rough around the edges' but enjoyable. Several like the words related to change. One gave you an 'F'—for 'fun'!"

"I think you guys now have a catchy and appropriate theme song," complimented Marla. "And, we'll fine-tune it to make it better. Can you believe, I'm finding it to be fun, too. Welcome change from school," she added.

"But now you have to pay your dues," she laughed. "We do have a school concert coming up, and your quartet would be a welcome addition. Good promotion for the concert, too as you get known via the radio."

"Sounds hunky-dory," answered Steve, "if I'm allowed to speak for all."

"Thanks for your agreeable response," said Marla, as she noted the signs of agreement from the others.

Chapter 14: Away in I-O-Way

Krag realized that several weeks had gone by since the visit from the University folks, and he had not yet arranged to visit the Deere headquarters. Dr. Kay had been away from her office much of the summer but expected to be back now. High time to take her up on her willingness to accompany him to Moline. Maybe they could swing through the Cedar Rapids area to check out some more paintings by Grant Wood. She too, seemed to be well informed about those rural scenes.

After her bland answer on the phone, she brightened when she heard Krag's voice.

"I've been out of touch with your news," Kay said initially. "Haven't heard any reports about mysterious fires," said Kay. "Hope all is quiet on the home-front...and the *Homestead*."

"Coincidental. Accidental. We're not sure," said Krag. "But the 4th of July had some extra fireworks. A farmer not far from here had been restoring an old truck. Left it in a field when it died and wouldn't start again. Now it sure won't start again, because it exploded during the night. Investigators couldn't figure out why, until the latest postcard arrived, covered with soot. According to the message, the firebug had used a 'punk.' You know, the kind that smolders slowly and is used to light firecrackers. It probably lit fireworks in a delayed reaction, then the gas of the truck."

"Oh yeah! I've used punks," said Kay. "They burn for quite a while. Better—and safer—than using matches to light firecrackers."

"Obviously what the firebug thought too," said Krag.

"Now, back to the reason I called. I thought I'd better live up to my intent, or my hope anyway, to enlist you as my consort again, to visit the dramatic new headquarters of Deere."

"Still a 'yes,'" said Kay.

"Perfect answer," chuckled Krag.

"Maybe," said Kay, "if time permits, we could swing by Cedar Rapids on the way back and take in more of the Grant Wood art...at the museum and scattered in other places in the city. And if Grant Wood still beckons, we can cruise over to Davenport another time for more of his art."

"Great!" Krag responded with enthusiasm. "I was just thinking about that. It will expand my appreciation of Iowa. And my appreciation for you."

"Aha," laughed Kay. "Well, I admit, I do enjoy the flattery."

"Compliment, not flattery," protested Krag.

"Now, about our visit to Deere," said Krag. "According to what I read about the grand opening of the headquarters, the structure is distinctive, overlooking a small lake.

"Designed by one of my favorites, Eero Saarinen, who used some special steel that rusts to a rich brown—and stays that color. Reviewers called it an 'earthy' look. Certainly fitting for an ag company.

"Dramatic interior bathed in natural light. Again, appropriate for the prairie horizons, I'd conclude," said Krag.

Deere headquarters

"I've been tracking the progress at Deere too," Kay indicated. "Sad to think that Saarinen died before the completion of the building," she said. "He never got to see how the weathering set the color of the building."

"We'll get a grand tour by the marketing manager, starting with lunch in the new dining room," said Krag. "Of course, I'll be interested in the latest climate control in that building."

"I hope I can get some insights related to the steady evolution of agriculture, with farm equipment a revealing barometer," Kay commented. "Machinery getting bigger and small farms fading."

"That sure fits my concern," said Krag. "Everything about farming now points to big business, from investing to marketing, and a lot of giant steps in between.

Thorstein Veblen

"My family gave in to the inevitable conclusion that we, including me, couldn't farm the land acquired by our grandparents. So it went to the highest bidder."

"I know that from personal experience, as well as academic analysis," said Kay. "I grew up with diversified farming in Minnesota, focused on our family's dairy business.

"Our local co-op creamery served as a significant step in that change. Now the headquarters of the huge Land O' Lakes co-op is not far from our farm.

"And, by the way, the Nerstrand farm of that exceptional Veblen family that you're keen about was not far away from our place. And the same for Carlton College in Northfield, where Thorstein Veblen started his roller-coaster academic and marital life."

"Aha," Krag responded. "A glimmer into your former life. I look forward to learning more."

"Hope we can have some interesting sharing," answered Kay, "while we cruise to Moline—in your Winnebago, I suppose. You did confess that your Tucker is for show, so I won't expect that. What a disappointment!" laughed Kay.

"I'll surprise you with another vehicle," said Krag. "I think you'll like it. Even has some thermal-control parts from our company."

"I won't try to guess right now," laughed Kay. "But I'll be wondering."

Later, back at KRRL, Jim shouted: "Hail, hail, the gang's all here!" as his broadcast session indicated that the team had arrived again. "Thanks for rounding them up, Marla."

"I've been tuning them up too, so to speak," said Marla. "We're about ready to record their theme song so you can promote these 'barber-shoppers' on the air. They seem to be developing quite a following, and not just here.

"And we're expanding their repertoire. Maybe take them on the road for some local gigs," continued Marla. "More opportunity to promote the Iowa of the future. With old-time barbershop songs," she laughed.

"Thanks to your notoriety with notes," chuckled Jim, "my business is booming too. So keep on keeping-on! Maybe we should conduct a contest to name your quartet. Generate more interest. They've just been sort of anonymous so far."

"Hey Krag, speaking of tuning up," said Mike, "we've got your Avanti ready for the road. Our guys enjoyed sprucing up that gold color, so you'll be sure to impress your girlfriend in Ames."

"What's this about his 'girlfriend?'" exclaimed Marla. "I had my eye on him!"

"Now you tell me," laughed Krag.

"She's a tall, blond and beautiful college professor," explained Steve. "She's a bit aloof, but I think Krag is enchanted by her."

"He's going a-courtin', you might say," said Steve as he jumped into the 'gossip' with the other Cupids. And he began singing "Froggie Went A-Courtin'." And the others, including Marla, joined in.

"Wait a minute!" exclaimed Marla, with a laugh. "I don't want Krag to 'go a-courtin', when I'm right here."

"Oh yeah, real courtin'," laughed Krag. "Dr. Kay and I are going to visit the new headquarters of Deere at Moline. And to Cedar Rapids to see more art by Grant Wood. How's that for romantic. We'll focus on her specialty of 'rural economics' with the marketing executive at Deere."

"Dear me!" responded Marla. "When do I get to meet my 'fem fatale' competitor?"

"At your Fall high- school concert," offered Krag. "Though I might need your help in enticing her to come down here."

"Count on it," said Marla. "I want to see what she's got that I ain't got!"

"Me too," said Mike. "I'd say that you measure-up mighty well. But an in-person comparison will be a treat for the eyes."

"Maybe Krag can take a turn at being Cupid too," suggested Steve. "The University must enroll lots of eligible grad students who might fit your style and quality better than any Grund candidates."

"You're too special to waste locally," he added, as Marla chuckled.

"Thanks for your unusual but genuine compliment," she responded, still chuckling.

When the time came for Krag to head out, several others besides the three from the quartet and Jim came to send him off. The rest of the gapers came to see the rare Avanti. And Marla announced that she had skipped school so she could see this "gold bug" sports car. So had some of her students.

At the roar of the engine, Mike and his "pit crew" signaled a "thumbs up" as Krag pointed the Avanti north.

Avanti

A short time later, the secretary in the Rural Economics office welcomed Krag with a warm smile. Others nearby offered a similar silent greeting.

Kay came out of her office when alerted about an "important visitor." She smiled and shook hands and led Krag into her office.

"Okay to hug, now that we are secluded?" asked Krag, who hugged Kay without waiting for an answer. He kissed her on the forehead when she hugged him back.

"Seems like old times," he laughed, "even though this is only the third time we've been together. And the first time may not count, because you were incognito as a spy."

"Let's go out in the open," Kay suggested, with another smile. "Before we hit the road, we can have a cup of coffee at our conference table, so others can meet you too. They're waiting with bated breath—and still harbor a degree of disbelief that you're real."

Then Phil and Frank strolled over to greet Krag and express their pleasure at seeing him again. And they broke the ice as several others introduced themselves.

"Well, Kay, what kind of exotic vehicle did he drive today?" pondered Phil.

"Didn't get a chance to see," she admitted.

"Definitely not your run-of-the-mill University sedan," said Frank. "I saw it when he drove up. Any hints to help Kay in guessing?"

"Rural America for sure," said Krag. "By a company that used to make Conestoga wagons."

"A Studebaker!" exclaimed Kay. "Special, you said, Krag. So I bet it's an Avanti!"

"Good deduction, Sherlock," said Krag. "And that earns you a free ride all the way to Illinois!"

"Ready when you are," said Kay, with a wave to the group. "Let's take a look at the Avanti!"

As they left the office area, Phil grinned and whispered to Frank: "I think there's mutual interest in more than a car and tractor."

Chapter 15: A Plow for the Prairie

Checking the time, Krag and Kay decided to leave the Grant Wood tour of Cedar Rapids till their return to Ames.

"Maybe before our meeting, we can go through the museum that's part of the new Deere headquarters," suggested Kay.

"Sounds good, for our schedule...and my edification," said Krag.

"And mine," added Kay.

At the entrance, the receptionist alerted the marketing manager by phone about their arrival. "They're early for your meeting, your guests said, so they will use the extra time to visit our museum."

Deere museum

"Good opportunity for a refresher about the company," said Kay as they entered the museum.

From the plaque about the founder, Krag compared timing about his great-grandfather's arrival in America. "Looks like my side was at least a generation later than John Deere. He sure displayed some practical approaches to farming," as he noted John Deere's modification of the plow-share. "So they 'shared' interest in improvements."

"Oh no!" exclaimed Kay. "A pun so early!"

"Remarkable link between the qualities of the steel in his father's tailoring needles, to the need for polished smoothness so the Deere plow could turn the sticky clay of the Midwest.

"His adaptability and dedication to quality certainly set the standards for the company's future," Krag said, with admiration.

"And I'm eager to learn more about how those characteristics fit the current trends of change that we're exploring at the University," Kay stated, "and that you're calling attention to in your radio campaign."

In their meeting with the marketing manager, they learned that research related to the past and present in agriculture, particularly to Deere, was steering the company toward the future. Bigger equipment, advanced controls, energy efficiency, and greater creature comfort for operators of the machines. Manufacturing improvements included greater precision of parts and more efficient assembly, with the help of robotics and electronics.

Yes, Krag learned, the electronic controls from his company fit with the operating and energy efficiency of the Deere products.

When the marketing manager switched gears to inquire about the unusual vandalism near Des Moines he had heard about, Krag told about his advocacy for positive change in Iowa—and that the reaction to the radio program at KRRL wasn't always positive. "But we don't have proof of any connection to our advocacy of change to vandalism, just suspicions.

"Maybe, regarding our program on KRRL," suggested Krag, "your company would be interested in advertising on that station."

"I've heard good reports about your program and your barbershop singers. In fact, we might want to bring your barbershop quartet here to sing at our annual shareholders' meeting in May. We should draw a big crowd, especially with our new building, and we offer food and entertainment. Could be fun to have you here! So we'll be in touch."

 After that a guide took them on a tour of the building and grounds, and concluded by telling them about the lunch menu and seating area—suggesting a table with a view of the pond on one side of the building.

Then they learned that the guide is a student from Chicago.

"Erica Hallin," she said. "Pronounced with the accent on the second syllable, and the 'i' as 'ee'," she explained. Then she laughed as she realized the two Scandinavian visitors would know that. "I'm a student at nearby Augustana College in Rock Island," she continued. "From Chicago."

Then she and Krag talked about the Andersonville section of Chicago, with its Swedish and other Scandinavian connections. Kay chimed in with her reactions about a visit there. They all agreed that the ethnic enclaves such as Andersonville are changing and shrinking.

Kay suggested that Erica consider graduate study at Iowa State, so she gave the student a business card and urged her to stay in touch, especially if she leaned toward issues related to rural life.

Krag added his hope of helping Midwesterners adapt to the ongoing changes that are affecting the area.

"As I assume you know," explained Erica, "we are in the Quad Cities, which are divided by the Mississippi, with Rock Island and Moline on the Illinois side, and Davenport and Bettendorf over in Iowa."

"This agricultural and industrial area," said Kay, "is like the changes on the other side of Iowa, with Council Bluffs on the Iowa side of the Missouri River and Omaha across in Nebraska.

"Now here on the Mississippi, barges ply the river instead of the log rafts of the past. Hardly the quaint traffic that Mark Twain would have seen," she added, with a smile.

"A conspicuous example of the flow of change," agreed Krag.

"Looks as though we can still swing by the Cedar Rapids art museum on our way back," said Kay after they finished their delicious and nutritious lunch. "There we will learn more about rural economics from the art of Grant Wood. About education, too, from his painting of a one-room country school—like where I started."

"Hard to imagine," Krag said in surprise. "You've certainly come a long way, and without the education advantages I had in Chicago. We had great learning opportunities, enriched by cultural and other extra-curricular activities. Sure hard to imagine the limits of your situation."

"Surprisingly," Kay countered, "the teacher I had for all eight years educated, and inspired me and the other kids, with her skill and support.

"Our school, like the painting we'll see, now exists as a museum. Maybe you'd like to go there some day, to the town of Canute where I went to high school. And to our farm where you can meet what's left of my family living there."

"Plan on it!" he said with a smile, "to quote you when you agreed earlier to be my consort today."

Before they crossed the Mississippi River into Iowa, Kay pointed out the campus of Augustana College. "Hope to see Erica again someday," she said.

As they passed a campus building, Kay added, "The future you are pondering will need many like Erica to lead in those changes."

Augustana College

At the Cedar Rapids art museum, they soaked up the varied art of Grant Wood and other Regionalists.

To rest their feet and brain from art overload, they paused for coffee and conversation in the museum's cafeteria to reflect about the paintings that captured the past.

"Have to hand it to someone like John Deere!" Krag declared as he thought about the significance of basic developments such as Deere's plow that was adapted for the challenges of the prairie.

"In the spirit of the Midwest, he kept learning and experimenting.

"He didn't count on academic classes and formal research, but practical understanding of farming and ingenious solutions to problems.

"The Deere Company museum sure is a great showcase of the progress in agriculture!"

Thinking about Krag's information, Kay commented, "In that way, he reminds me of another outstanding experimenter from the Midwest," if you'll pardon my changing players.

Norman Borlaug

"Norman Borlaug grew up in Iowa, even went to a one-room country school like I did. And studied at the University of Minnesota, like I did. Got his PhD there too. Now he's been leading the way in genetics and plant pathology to maximize the hardiness and food value of agricultural plants. Mexico is just one place his research has helped save people from starvation."

"Too bad Grant Wood didn't paint Borlaug's portrait," commented Krag. "Certainly a worthy subject...and a man after Wood's own heart, I would conclude.

"Maybe I should try to recruit Dr. Borlaug to be a spokesman for our campaign about change."

"That would divide your cause between plaudits and protests," Kay surmised. "Hope for progress would get support, but genetic change would worry many—even though such genetic shifts have occurred gradually for centuries.

"Now, are you rested and ready for more art?" asked Kay. "In the spirit of planting, we can look at Grant Wood's tribute to Arbor Day with some school kids planting a tree."

"As you no doubt know, Congress expanded the original Homestead Act by offering free land as an incentive for tree-planting," said Krag. "So our family planted trees, and kept on planting with an orchard and gardens, to the dismay of my dad and his sibs, who tended that crop…until they eventually escaped to the city.

"Now, the others in my clan were glad to sell the place, but were willing to let me buy the buildings of the *Homestead*. Memories of all the chores came with it. Actually, I enjoy the place, and find that it serves as a form of renewal."

Arbor Day by **Grant Wood**

"Okay, let's make another round of the museum and look at whatever else we find along the way," said Krag. "Then I'd better take you back to Ames."

"Sounds good. And imagine this situation, if you can," said Kay after they viewed the painting of tree-planting at a country school... a significant and formative part of my life."

Back in Ames, Krag asked: "Your office or your home? Or do you need to pick up your car at the University?"

"It's late enough that my office will be closed. So, it's 'Home, Jeeves'! I live close enough that I seldom drive, unless I need the car for some reason at the end of the day."

Krag followed her directions—then he asked suddenly: "Maybe you'd like an early dinner? I should have asked that before. Any suggestions?"

"There's a little 'mom & pop' diner near my place. I eat there regularly, and they treat me like I'm part of the family," Kay suggested. "Want to try another taste of rural Iowa...even if this isn't as rural as your community?"

"Sure do! Probably be similar to what Annicka might cook for me," said Krag. "Besides, I hate to have this day come to an end."

"Don't know if this will meet the standards of Annicka's picnic fare, but the place will be warm and friendly like your picnic," Kay explained. "Here we are. Park right in front and give others a chance to admire your Avanti."

Inside, "Mom" greeted her...them. "Got a new car...and new boyfriend?" she smiled.

"Well," Kay delayed responding, "not really, but this is my friend Krag Jensen, and that fancy car is his."

Then "Pop" came over to greet them. "I heard your answer," he laughed, "and I'd say 'keep 'em both'! Think he'd like your dinner special?"

"I count on it!" said Krag. "What's good for her is good for me!"

"Okay, two orders of broiled salmon, with a buttered baked potato plus sour cream, and a green salad on the side," Pop called out. "Hard wheat-roll. Custard dessert. And coffee."

Before they could sit at the designated booth, two co-eds and their boyfriends greeted them. "Nice to see you, Dr. Arnesen," said one coy co-ed. "Our friends do wonder what that sleek car is that you came in."

Others in the café tuned in as she informed them: "A Studebaker Avanti—but he won't let me drive it," she said as if pouting, as she looked at Krag. "Afraid I might scratch it!"

"Give her a chance! We can vouch for her as a skilled driver," said the co-ed to Krag, as other 'regulars' in the café echoed the statement, and some just nodded.

"Okay, you win, Dr. Arnesen...next week will be your turn to drive," declared Krag, as all in the cafe clapped in approval.

Then he gallantly took her hand and led her to the booth. In the booth, he still held her hand as they both chuckled about the reactions of the other patrons.

"You're devious, making me an ogre," he laughed, as she smiled. "But I tricked you too, because now we have a date for next week, so you can drive the Avanti. And where to, I might ask? To Knute to visit your past?"

"That would be fun," she said. "Let me see if I can arrange it. Maybe on the weekend. By the way, we have two syllables in our town's name, spelled C-A-N-U-T-E, so it's not confused with 'Nute' as some pronounce your spelling of the name."

After their relaxed meal, they headed for the Avanti, while Mom and Pop and other patrons waved farewell. At the Avanti, a phalanx of students waited to bid them good evening.

"You're a good influence," laughed Kay. "I've never got such a good response from students before. Guess I'll have to keep the Avanti."

"How about me?" wondered Krag.

"Depends on a lengthy test drive," said Kay. "Anyway," she announced a few minutes later, "here's my place, handy to the University, to the café, to stores, to entertainment."

"Let me walk you to your door," said Krag as he opened the Avanti door and held her hand as she got out.

At her apartment door, she squeezed his hand and murmured, "That was fun. Everything."

She turned and hugged him, and he kissed her on her forehead, then the tip of her nose, then on her lips. Then "Goodnight, and thanks," she said. "Time for me to go in," she added, with a slight quaver in her voice.

"Cold?" he asked.

"No...too warm," she laughed, as she opened the door and went in, leaving him standing there, a bit dazed.

Chapter 16: Homeward Bound

The next week for the scheduled rendezvous at Canute in Minnesota, Krag called to announce "I aims to be in Ames early Saturday morning...can catch breakfast along the way."

"Suits me fine," answered Kay, "except for the corny play on Ames. And, yes, I know of a breakfast stop on the way."

In her promised driver's seat, she looked over the Avanti's dashboard displays and the gear arrangement. "Four-speed with turbo-charged engine. Should be fun! Like my Mustang."

"You drive a Mustang!" responded a surprised Krag. "I'd like to take a turn at that."

"I believe it can be arranged," laughed Kay.

As they cruised north into Minnesota, Krag noticed a refreshing change from Iowa, with rolling, tree-covered hills. "Colorful sight, those deciduous trees with what's left of their leaves, contrasted by a mix of conifers. But I think my great-grandfather chose better land for farming."

"Depends on the farming," responded Kay. "The land around Canute suited our dairy business."

In their stop for breakfast in a small town, the Avanti attracted attention, as did the driver, indicated by the whistles from high school boys and smiles from the girls.

"What's the story behind the name 'Canute' for your town?" asked Krag.

"You know, the Danish hero, King Canute," explained Kay. "Spelled our way—C-a-n-u-t-e."

"Have to get used to that spelling, because I always thought of the king as 'K-n-u-t-e'," said Krag. "Or just 'K-n-u-t'."

"I suppose the early Danes thought the Americans couldn't pronounce it the old way, so Canute our way seemed logical," explained Kay.

"To help you can catch the spirit of the town," added Kay, "I'll have to bring you back the last week of the year—when school's out for Christmas vacation. Time for the 'Great Canute Days', when our town tries to hold back the blizzard."

"Oh yeah!" said Krag. "Like when King Knute of Denmark was expected—but failed—to hold back the tide! Hey, that symbolizes us, too, emphasizing that we can't hold back change!"

"Well, now Canute has become a tourist attraction with a cluster of stores selling antiques, mostly for the folks from the Twin Cities," explained Kay. "Actually, a lot of Twin Cities commuters live here now, and they add gusto and creativity to the 'Blizzard Battle'. The promoters even harvest ice blocks from the river and inject dye to create an iridescent fort. Snow sculpture, of course. But not quite up to the scale of the St. Paul Winter Carnival. The kids in particular enjoy the snow-ball fights and 'fox-and-geese' tag."

"Another part of 'rural economics', I suppose," smiled Krag.

On the road again, she declared that she felt like a race-car driver, handling sharp curves, braking and shifting.

"Be home soon," announced Kay. "Mom and Dad were surprised to hear I'd be bringing a friend. A male friend."

"I could enjoy sharing a room?" joked Krag, and then he apologized. "Sorry, that could be an unpleasant subject. When I wondered why you're still single, Phil alluded to a bad experience you had with a college professor."

"He sure took advantage of naïve me," lamented Kay. "Even though I had some sex education from the farm breeding lessons and from high school talk—girls and boys. But my professor led me to believe I was his chosen one as well as his favorite student assistant. So I was pliable and vulnerable. He was nice-looking and charming, skilled at seduction. And he served as my academic advisor, so he used academic extortion as another tactic to end my virginity."

"Sounds like characters right out of our Norse literature," recalled Krag. "Corrupt-and-married Erlend Nikulausson seduced young Kristin Lavransdattar, and worthless rover Peer Gynt strung along faithful Solveig."

"After my 'Erlend' completed his conquest," lamented a sorrowful Kay, "he dropped me like a hot potato and moved on to seducing other co-eds. Left me wary, bitter and feeling guilty. And now at age 36, an old-maid schoolteacher."

"Au contraire!" contradicted Krag. "Another example of change occurring all around us. Talented women now succeeding in challenging careers. And for you, beauty besides!"

"I could kiss you for that," she murmured.

"Please do!" he responded.

And she did—at the next stop sign.

"Don't stop that part though!" he said, as he—they—laughed.

Soon Kay waved at her country school. Then they passed an old-style gas station…with modern pumps. And tree-lined streets, past a brick school building, next the city hall and post office, then stores on Main Street.

"Makes me think of Sinclair Lewis," Kay stated.

"Yeah, when I was growing up in Chicago, he planted a picture of a small town in me," Krag recalled. "Not a pretty picture."

Then they took a turn…and a stop, at a house out of a Grant Wood painting. White picket fence, white house with white pillars on a porch…lined with people. Puzzled by the strange car.

But the kids ran out for a closer look. And then shouted "It's Aunt Kay!" The kids danced and jumped around Kay, and Krag smiled in understanding.

Kay began introductions: "Mom and Dad, meet Krag Jensen," as they smiled and shook hands. Brothers and sisters and in-laws added their greetings.

"Danish, I'd guess," said one.

"Right," he answered, "and from the town of Grundtvig in Iowa. And from Chicago, but I live on the *Homestead* founded by my great-grandfather."

An older niece whispered "Hubba-hubba" to her cousin as she admired tall and handsome Krag.

Another niece liked the car, but wondered what kind it is. An older nephew answered: "A Studebaker Avanti."

"Yours, Aunt Kay?" asked another.

"His," smiled Kay.

"What do you have?" asked another.

"A Mustang," replied Kay.

"Wow!" came a shared reaction.

"Getting a bit chilly out here," said Dad. "Time to go inside, and soon time for some supper."

Kay's older brother interrupted to say they had to be on their way. "Just wanted to say hello. If you're here for the weekend, we'll see you again before you leave."

He and his wife and kids hugged Kay and shook hands with Krag. Then others followed suit. "This will give Mom and Dad first chance to hear the latest from you," said Kay's sister.

During the "mashed potatoes & gravy" supper, Mom and Dad listened eagerly as Kay told about their visit to the Deere headquarters, and Krag told about his *Homestead*. And his KJ Industries.

"Sounds like our Honeywell company," said Kay's dad.

"We connect with them on-and-off with our controls," Krag said with a slight grin for his play on words, caught by Kay.

They could identify personally when Krag told about his Danish roots and his great-grandfather homesteading the land in Iowa after serving in the Union army. They expressed heartfelt sympathy as he told about the death of his wife and children in a plane crash.

Kay wiped away a tear at her thought that she had entered into Krag's life only after he had lost his family. And now he was helping her recover from her painful and lingering emotional trauma of years ago.

They all laughed after Krag sang the theme song of his KRRL radio program. And he told about how he encourages listeners to adapt to change in Iowa, in the country and in the world.

"Understood by most people, but not appreciated by all," he said. "Some see change as a threat to their way of life."

"We see it here," said her dad. "In our dairy business, in our community. Can't turn back, with progress nipping at our heels."

At bedtime, Kay showed Krag his room, "used by my brothers. And I'm next door, but don't you try sneaking in. Might be okay in modern Denmark, but not in this old-time Danish family."

"A goodnight kiss?" he inquired. She answered by hugging him tightly and kissing him warmly.

"Time to snuggle into bed," she said suddenly.

"Cold?" he asked.

"Too warm," she laughed.

The next morning for Kay and Krag began a Marathon of meeting and greeting people—in the stores, at a high school basketball game, worship at the Lutheran church, and off and on with various parts of Kay's family. Plus a visit to the family's barn to see modern dairy methods.

"Another example of change," said Krag as he noted the advanced equipment and procedures. "For the good...mostly."

Before they left, Kay announced that they'd be back soon. "I want to drag Krag back here to experience how Canute tries to hold back a blizzard.

The family and friends joined in the laughter.

With Krag back in the driver's seat, they headed south, both waving out the car windows until the family was out of sight.

"You got to experience the long goodbye that's part of the charm of a small town," smiled Kay. "Hope you enjoyed the visit."

"Sure did!" responded Krag. "Especially your wonderful family. The touch of Denmark added to my sense of belonging."

"Maybe another time we can drive farther north to Askov, Minnesota to take in the 'Rutabaga Festival & Fair'," laughed Kay. "Agriculture based on a species of rutabaga imported from Denmark. Then we could go west in the state to attend the Danish folk school in Tyler. "

"Askov...that rings a sports trivia bell with me," chuckled Krag. "A star of the Minneapolis Lakers came from that little town. Vern Mikklesen, I think."

"I suppose we can savor *aebleskiver* at those towns as well as in Canute," he said, hopefully.

"And, as I recall," said Kay, "at your *Homestead* too, so ably prepared, if you'll pardon the pun, by your talented chef Annicka."

As they entered Ames, Kay smiled as she put her hand on his as it rested on the gearshift knob. And he looked at her with a sparkle in his eyes.

"I do believe the colors of the leaves brightened over the weekend," said Krag, "and these rolling hills and river valleys were obviously created by Grant Wood."

When they reached her apartment building in Ames, Kay offered to fix a light supper before Krag headed for his *Homestead.*

"Thanks, that would be just the right kind of meal after our hearty farm dinners," answered Krag.

"You can relax," Kay suggested, "while I put together our soup and sandwich, and some fruit."

Looking around the small apartment, Krag noticed the simple furnishings, plus a radio, record player, small television set and a spinet piano. And a large and well-stocked book case.

"Shaker furniture?" he asked, as they sat at the dining table.

"In the arts and crafts style," she explained. "Dad and I worked together to create some of the pieces, like this table and the end tables there. Lamps too. But I bought the complementary sofa and chairs. "

"Handsome...and practical," commented Krag. "Do you like music to match as well?"

"Eclectic," she answered. "Classical—Anton Dvorak, for Iowa, of course—plus favorites such as Gershwin, Copeland and Grofé. Wait till you hear my recording of Lauritz Melchior. He booms through the whole building. My neighbor, a young music teacher and grad student, expressed some concern—not about the music, just the volume. I try to keep it down so I don't disturb him. Oh, I also have a rare piece of sheet music by Danish composer Carl Neilsen."

"Admirable!" Krag responded. "A far cry from our barbershop songs. I look forward to listening with you and to your playing. You can help me on our Danish heritage too."

"Okay," Kay laughed, "then it'll be my turn to listen…to you when you sing at the Deere Company annual meeting."

"Well before that, I hope," said Krag. "I promised our music director I'd try to bring you down for her Fall community concert, which will include our quartet.

"Marla Madsen's her name, and she keeps us on our toes, doing her best to help us improve. Teaches at the high school and is an outstanding musician herself. She wants to meet you, and I think you two would like each other.

"So, at Marla's urging, I hope you will set aside time to come our way just after Thanksgiving."

"Love to," confirmed Kay.

"Want me to come and get you?" asked Krag.

"Oh no, the Mustang can easily handle that drive," smiled Kay. "Besides, you'll be busy if you're in the program too."

"Now, it's time for me to hit the trail again, since I can say 'mission accomplished' by inviting you back to Grundtvig."

He held her hand as they walked to the door, then wrapped his arms around her. As she held him, he brushed her hair back with one hand and caressed her cheek. Then they kissed with passion.

When she felt his hardened penis pressed against her, she realized that now her past revulsion and guilt about sex was fading, and the embrace thrilled her.

He felt a shiver from her, and asked: "Cold?"

"No...very warm...so I'd better send you on your way!"

Chapter 17: Threat Continues

A rolling fire in a round hay bale led to a personalized threat on the latest postcard from Des Moines:

Round hay bale, created by your Iowa State bunch, made dramatic rolling torch to K's torch."

A crude red swirl signed the card.

The barbershop quartet was due for another program, when Jim called them and Marla to meet ahead of time for the latest fire incident. He said he had already alerted authorities, who knew about the hay bale that had been set afire and shoved down a hill...but ended harmlessly in a ravine.

In the discussion about the latest incident, they pondered about the Iowa State reference.

"I think I know," said Steve, "because I recall that two scientists from Iowa State University developed that process recently. Those round bales weight a ton, so to speak, so the burning bale must have been teetering at the top of a rise to be pushed."

"Looks like the writer refers to your romance with your professor—your torch," said Marla, with a hint of sarcasm.

"But how does the firebug know about the Iowa State University connection?" wondered Krag.

"Well," responded Marla, "with all the fanfare when we sent you off in your fancy Avanti to Ames, you became the focus of a bit of gossip. And other radio stations are sharing your story, not to mention the newspapers in Des Moines and Omaha and Council Bluffs, as well as our local *Sower*."

"I got wind of a rumor that the TV station in Des Moines wants to interview our bunch, particularly you, Krag," said Steve. "Partly because Iowa prides itself on the development of the round hay bales, the role of Iowa State scientists would be well known for that development."

"Looks like all we can do is keep our eyes and ears open for any clues," said Jim. "So the next question goes to you, Marla. How are the boys shaping up?"

"Still not ready to be in *The Music Man*," said Marla, "but growing in quality—and quantity in their repertoire."

"Remember our idea of a naming contest," said Jim, "we decided you guys suggested that we suggest three names of your group for our listeners to choose from. Time to get on with it, but we don't want the contest to be wide open. No telling what awful names our listeners might suggest, so we'll let them chose from our acceptable three. Good promotion, whichever one wins!"

"The *Warblers*...lots of those birds around," said Harry.

"Or the *Cruisers*," added Mike, "Ties in with our Winnie."

"And last, but not least, I hope," said Marla, "the *Clef Dwellers*, to emphasize your special music."

"Okay, if no one objects," declared Jim, with a grin, "let's run it up the flagpole—or antennae, and find out what our discerning listeners prefer."

"Do we offer prizes?" asked Mike.

"Maybe a gift card from the music store we patronize in Des Moines," Jim suggested. "Perhaps better than a framed photo of you guys," he chuckled. "Although, with Marla in the picture, that might be appealing after all."

And the other men grinned in agreement.

"Flatterers, maybe that should be the name of this group," laughed Marla. "You seem to lay it on thick when I get too tough with you."

After the program of the day, Krag intercepted Marla before she left. "My torch, sometimes known as Dr. Arnesen, wants to come down for your Fall concert. She's quite knowledgeable about music, so you might find a good shared interest."

"Such as you," smiled Marla. "Still, if you like her, I think I will too."

Before he left the station, Krag called his "torch."

She answered, with a smile in her voice, and she laughed when he told she had another and new name, the "torch."

Then, he explained the incident about the round bale being burned, and the card that implied that it tied in with K's "torch", "meaning me and you, of course," Krag warned.

"Beware, some reporter will probably identify you as the 'torch', so you might want to be ready to explain your 'burning desire' for me," laughed Krag.

In a more serious tone, he added, "your department might also want to be on guard," continued Krag, "because the postcard also implied that the round-bale concept developed at Iowa State University might be an example of more undesirable change in Iowa."

"Bizarre!" said an astonished Kay. "First, how did the card writer know about us and then the strange link of the round bale to the University?"

"Seems like the Avanti got attention in our community, too, and the association with you generated gossip, which I don't object to. But now we're increasingly more watchful about the risk of fire," said Krag. "The state fire marshal and even the FBI have become interested.

"But to the good news," Krag continued. "I told our music director Marla that I invited you to her Fall concert, and she looks forward to talking about music with you. And maybe about us too," he teased."

"Sounds...enjoyable...and interesting..." allowed Kay, "and a welcome chance to be with you again! But don't count on that 'burning desire'!"

Back at the Homestead, Krag encountered an agitated Annicka.

"News gets around," she explained, "and now I learned that the firebug has included you in the threats. I've got my shotgun ready just in case," she added, as she showed him her double-barrelled shotgun. "If it's good enough for pheasants, it should take care of a firebug too."

"Do you mean that the special fowl-feast you prepare is really pheasant...shot out of season?" asked a laughing Krag.

"They're always in season when they invade my garden," she answered, "and I only shoot roosters. The hens keep the supply growing."

"I hadn't thought about having a gun in this quiet community," Krag added, thoughtfully. "But now I'm glad you're armed, because that firebug seems to be getting bolder."

"Our community doesn't seem so quiet now," countered Annicka, "with the weird fires and now reporters snooping around. I suppose they'll try to track you down here—so should I be ready to answer their questions if you aren't around?"

"Well, you could tell them about our barbershop quartet, now officially called the *Warblers* as chosen by listeners in our naming contest.

Warbler

"Be sure to mention that the *Warblers* praise Iowa progress on KRRL. And that we sing superbly and are loved by all the radio listeners. And yes, you could say that we will be hosting Dr. Arnesen when she comes from Ames to enjoy the concert to be conducted by Marla Madsen. A reporter might want to interview Dr. Arnesen, because, as you know, she has been named as my 'torch'."

"Hold on!" exclaimed Annicka. "Let me take all that in. Such as Dr. Arnesen staying here, and that a reporter might want to interview her...and me. And you mentioned your listeners voted for your name. *Warblers*, I like that too."

"Well, you will have to monitor Dr. Kay's visit here, to make sure I don't get involved in any hanky-panky," laughed Krag. "And if a reporter interviews you, don't tell him that you shoot pheasants...out of season."

When Krag called Kay with details about the concert and said that she could stay at the *Homestead*, she expressed appreciation that she wouldn't have to drive back to Ames at night. And, she added, she will be bringing another music enthusiast—her neighbor, the grad student who also teaches music.

"His name is William Strom—as in 'strum the guitar'," she laughed. "He said he would not only expect to enjoy the concert, including your quartet, but also learn about such a community event for his research. And he would probably like to interview your friend Marla about her music as part of his graduate study.

"So could you accommodate one more guest at the *Homestead*?" asked Kay.

"Oh sure," laughed Krag. "There goes my hope to have you here alone for some hanky-panky!"

"Not a chance anyway," answered Kay, with mirth in her voice, "after you made up the comment that I harbor a 'burning desire' for you! Besides, I'm older and wiser now."

"Well, I have just one other warning for you," said Krag. "The news folks seem to be getting curiouser and curiouser about our community and our quartet and the fires and even the concert. So they might try to track you down to interview you when you visit here."

"Thanks for the 'heads up' about reporters," Kay responded. "Gives me time to anticipate questions and think of answers, just in case."

Later at KRRL, before their program, Jim and the quartet and Marla celebrated the voters' choice of the *Warblers* as their new name.

"We got a huge response of cards and letters!" said an enthusiast Jim. "Some other stations would like have you *Warblers* share your program, and I don't see why not. It will be good for the future of Iowa, and good for your hope to go on the road with your show."

"Great to hear!" said Krag, as the others nodded agreement.

After the program, Krag snagged Marla before she left so he could tell her about visitors coming from Ames.

"I thought you said just one visitor, your 'Torch'," said a puzzled Marla.

"Another musician wants to come along to take in the concert as part of his own teaching and his graduate research," explained Krag. "His name is William Strom, and he hopes to talk with you about your role in music here. He will also stay at the *Homestead* after your concert, so maybe then we could all get together there to celebrate the community musical milestone."

"Sounds like fun…and a chance for me to learn from another teacher," said Marla.

"I alerted Kay that reporters have been snooping around to learn about our community and may want to snag folks, such as Kay and you, for interviews," Krag explained.

"Information about the postcards hasn't been released, except to the police. But that may have leaked, so reporters might know about communication from the firebug."

"Okay, time to put my 'thinking cap' on," reacted Marla. "About all of this—our radio program and its purpose, about your 'torch,' the visiting music teacher and possible questions from reporters. Maybe the media will even show interest in our concert, we hope."

Chapter 18: Identity Clues

"The bug is back!" exclaimed Jim before the start of the next *Warblers* program. "As you know from the wide news coverage in our community these days of mysterious fires, the firebug created a blaze in a box car rolling through town. Police and the fire department that extinguished the fire are baffled about how it could have started with no one in sight."

"So far," said a relieved Harry, "the firebug hasn't set fires that have harmed people. But that's no guarantee for the future."

"Strange targets," pondered Mike. "That old truck burned using a punk for a delayed lighting of fireworks. Then a special birthday candle as a delayed fire-starter in the haystack. Next a rolling fire in the hay bale. And now in a moving box car. They seem random rather than for a purpose, but the purpose might be to scare the daylights out of us."

"The bug now wants to bug us with another puzzle," said Jim, scratching his head. "The postcard says:

Check story about fire by American escapee—now by escapee in America."

"Okay, group-think here," said Krag. "Let's try to come up with stories about fires. A movie I think of immediately is *Our Vines Have Tender Grapes*, because the barn burns. No connection with a prisoner, though."

"Makes me think of *Barn Burning,* the story by Faulkner," offered Steve. "But we can rule that out as the firebug's inspiration. No prisoner or box-car in that story."

"The story and movie *Come and Get It* was about logging and may have had a forest fire in it. And probably a rail-car, but not a prisoner that I recall," said Harry.

"Guess I should be able to come up with some stories about burning cars, like a prison-escape scene, but I can't come up with a name," said Mike. "Maybe I'll have to be hypnotized to help me remember."

"My turn in this group-think," Marla spoke up. "I recall a movie about American prisoners in Germany during the war. Give me a minute to try to remember the name, then you guys can fill in if you can."

"From the postcard, that might fit," considered Krag. "American prisoner—then prisoner of America."

"Now I remember," said Marla, "it was the movie *Stalag 17,* and one American prisoner reported how he had thrown a delayed fire bomb into a moving rail car. He made a fuse by lighting one match and sticking it in at the edge of a book of matches."

"Yeah, yeah!" exclaimed Krag. "Can't forget William Holden and Peter Graves in that movie," he added. "So simple, delaying lighting the book of matches to conceal the source."

"Now what does it mean?" pondered Jim.

"Hang on, something's clicking in the back of my mind about war prisoners," muttered Krag.

"Maybe this fits," he continued. "When I was in the Navy at the Great Lakes, someone who claimed to be a Danish ally later turned out to be a Nazi soldier. About the time he had convinced us he was Danish, he tried to drown me by disconnecting my air hose during an underwater exercise in Lake Michigan. I was saved, and Hans Schreiber was identified as a Nazi and convicted of attempted murder… to be sent with other Germans to a prison farm.

"But Shreiber was in the custody of a Navy ensign, the ensign added a preliminary punishment. The Danish-German was towed at high speed behind a boat. Nearly drowned him. The ensign compared it to well-deserved keel-hauling—the punishment meted out on old sailing ships.

"Maybe after all these years, that Danish-German wants revenge. He might have gone back to impersonating a Dane so he could blend into this Danish community."

"Could be a long shot," said Steve, "but it's about the only story that might fit."

"Hey, I just thought of another angle!" exclaimed Marla, almost shouting.

"We have a strange guy who's a night janitor at school. He hobbles around in his work. Hunched over like Quasimodo—which might be a disguise. Doesn't say anything. Just talks Danish with a few from town who drop by to chat. Maybe he got the job because other folks consider him Danish."

"Good detective thinking," praised Krag. "Right out of Edgar Allen Poe. Or Sherlock Holmes. Or Victor Hugo."

"Maybe the constables should check on him," suggested Jim. "They'd need to have someone along who can speak Danish...or German."

"Go ahead and arrange it," said Krag, as the others agreed.

Later, Krag called Kay to confirm the *Homestead* visit.

"Should be fun...and exciting!" exclaimed Kay. "I'm beginning to feel at home at the *Homestead*," she laughed.

"We are already planning a post-concert gathering at the *Homestead*," Krag shared. "Should be a good opportunity for your neighbor William to assess the event and get acquainted with us ordinary folks."

"Oh yeah, ordinary!" scoffed Kay. "The climate-control king basking in his comfort zone, restoring his *Homestead*, crusading for progress and branching out into entertainment."

"It does sound good, doesn't it!" laughed Krag.

"Indeed it does," Kay declared. "Except for that cloud of smoke hanging over you and your community. So what's new with the firebug?"

"The firebug posed a puzzle in the latest postcard," said Krag. "Referred to an American war prisoner and an implied link to a prisoner in America. But how, we wondered, did that relate to a fire? So we put our heads together—or butted them against a wall—until Marla remembered the movie *Stalag 17* and the simple method used for starting a fire with a book of matches.

"Well, I'll give you more details later. Too much to spell out now. But we are checking out a school worker who's raised Marla's suspicions. Acts like a Dane, but may be that German prisoner Hans Schreiber I tangled with years ago.

Days later, when Kay and William arrived at the *Homestead* in Kay's Mustang, Kay kissed Krag immediately and firmly.

Then she asked about the latest fire mysteries he had alluded to. "You really left me hanging," she scolded, but with warmth.

"Oh-oh, show time! I'll explain later," said Krag. "Let's park your gear in the house and hustle over to the school auditorium. We *Warblers* have to tune up. But we've reserved seats for the two of you. And I'll fill in some blanks after the concert when we share more at the *Homestead*," added Krag.

Before the concert at the school, he directed Kay and William to their seats.

Both of them sat entranced by the performance of students plus several community participants singing, declaiming and dancing with gusto. Marla, lively and lovely, enchanted both of them—Kay with a bit of jealousy and William with more than a bit of attraction.

Marla also directed the *Warblers,* who began with their theme song—interrupted by a burst of applause—and continued with a rousing imitation of the barbershop quartet from *The Music Man.*

To finish, she announced, that the *Warblers* would sing a hymn written by the town's namesake, Bishop Grundtvig. Like our theme song, his *Bright and Glorious Is the Sky* illuminates the Iowa sky at this Christmas time.

"I'm sure many of you Danes know that song, so join in and sing for joy!" declared Marla with a wave of her director's arms.

In a rewarding surprise for Marla, several reporters—including one from the Des Moines TV station—did cover the event. But their interest was split between the concert and the firebug mystery.

Just after the concert, the crowd as well as the reporters exited to a shocking sight in the town square. The Christmas tree, erected at the end of November, had turned into a flaming tower.

Though quickly doused by the fire department volunteers who were in the concert audience, the burning tree had completely captured the attention of the concert-goers and the reporters.

The TV camera crew skilfully switched from the interview of the performers to focus on the spectacle of the fire. And radio and newspaper reporters hastily interviewed the google-eyed onlookers.

Later, at the *Homestead,* the post-concert gathering gradually calmed as they began to enjoy the food and beverages offered by Annicka and her assistants from the Lutheran church.

Marla hugged Kay and laughed, "You look as lovely as Krag bragged.

"In our *Warbler* conversations, I learned that you had a bad previous relationship, so I hope that knowing Krag will offset that."

"It already has," Kay responded, "and thanks for your understanding."

"I've been there, with a fellow musician I loved," Marla shared. "When I went to Juilliard on a scholarship, he took the opportunity to have an affair with another musician. "

"So sorry," said Kay. "I know how it hurts."

"Perhaps it was good that his true character came out when it did," Marla added softly.

"Well," smiled Kay, "I just happened to bring a possible antidote. See William over there. He's a friendly neighbor in my apartment building. Teaches music in the Ames school system and is working on a master's degree. So busy that's he's still single…and available, as far as I know."

"Hmmm, handsome, too," laughed Marla.

"Let me introduce the two of you," suggested Kay.

Marla and William hit it off immediately, as she declared that she wanted to know his scholarly reactions to the concert. William was more than pleased to meet her, and enthusiastically shared with her his impressions of the performance.

When the time came for Marla to head for home, she asked William if he would keep her company as she walked home. The request startled him, but he wasted little time in agreeing to be her "protector." He and Marla talked as they walked the four blocks to her small house—about careers and music.

"Couldn't let you walk home alone after that fire," commented William.

"You're gallant to escort me home!" she said, with a twinkle in her eye, and she kissed him on the cheek as she opened her door. "I'll stop by in the morning at the *Homestead*, so we can talk when I'm not so keyed up by the concert. Besides, Annicka sets out a great breakfast."

On his way back to the *Homestead,* William felt frustrated. Marla looked so appealing and seemed so vibrant that he wished he could have wrapped arms around her and kissed her. Maybe someday, he hoped.

As he came in the door, William saw that Krag had his arms around Kay, so he waved and headed up the stairs to his bedroom.

"He looks almost as excited as you are," giggled Kay as she snuggled against Krag on the couch in front of the fireplace. "Strange, how this fire seems so comforting."

"Now, where were we?" murmured Krag.

"Before you waved 'goodnight' to William," answered Kay, "I believe your hand was sliding over my breast. I'll make it easier for you," she giggled, as she reached behind to unhook her bra.

He kissed her while he caressed each breast. "And I feel a delicate nipple rising and hardening," he murmured, with his voice coarsened by excitement.

"Oh! I feel something else hardening," she said, as she lay her hand on the swelling in his pants.

He gently pushed her down on the couch and rolled on top of her. They kissed and fondled, but he sensed her tenseness. So he sat up and raised her next to him again.

"Another time, another place, another situation," he said quietly.

"Yes, I'd like that," she said. "Now, I think, I should leave you with a 'goodnight' kiss. But I look forward to seeing you in the morning. Maybe you can tell me the rest of the story about the prisoner."

"I love you," he said.

"I know," she said. "And I do love you too, my dear Krag."

The next morning, Annicka lived up to her reputation with a breakfast layout to please all—Krag, Kay, Marla, William, and Jim, Harry, Mike and Steve.

"Okay, okay!" said Krag, with hands up in surrender. "Before you ask, Kay, here's our complicated prisoner scenario."

Then the KRRL team shared parts of the firebug theory, including Marla's 'Quasimodo' suspicions about the school janitor.

"I hate to think it," said a concerned Kay, "but all this seems to point to you, Krag, as the target. So beware, and be careful...please."

Then Kay switched the focus of the conversation, as she brought out a large, flat container.

"I assume you all know—except you, William—that Krag harbors a crazy idea to create a modern office and garage inside his barn.

"He had asked Frank, of the Architecture/Engineering Department at Iowa State, to turn that idea into reality."

She opened the box and lifted the top drawing for all to see.

"So here it is, a modern glass box with all the accoutrements for an efficient state-of-the-art office.

"It's stacked on top of a climate-controlled garage for Krag's toys. You know, his tractors, the Avanti, the Tucker, plus a practical vehicle or two."

"Wow, that is spectacular!" exclaimed Marla, as the others shared their enthusiastic appreciation.

"Frank thought these drawings would get you started in reviewing your needs, Krag. And your desires. Then you can meet with him and his staff at the University, so they can box you in with style."

Lifting up other sheets from the container, she explained that the additional drawings support the concept with a wide range of details.

"Just super!" exclaimed Krag. "Super! And now I'm really itching to install that modern beauty in our old-time barn!"

"That barn has its own classic beauty," declared Marla, which also brought agreement from the others, including Krag.

"I hate to share a grim reminder," said a stern-faced Steve, "but we certainly must guard your precious barn from the firebug.

"Maybe that kind of target is too obvious, so we probably should watch for a less-conspicuous action. But revenge against you evidently has motivated the firebug all along, and perhaps the fires were meant to be a diversion to distract you personally, Krag."

"Ironically, the barn isn't ready yet for the installation of my heat-sensing controls," regretted Krag.

"Well, at least Ben Franklin's lightning rods will protect the barn from fire coming out of the clouds."

"Any word about your Quasimodo at school?" Krag asked Marla.

Then Kay and William both piped up at the same time, puzzled about the mysterious Quasimodo.

"I thought he was the hunchback of Notre Dame," said Kay.

"And I remembered being scared out of my skull by him when I was a kid," laughed William.

"Poor boy," chuckled Marla as she put her hand on William's shoulder.

"Here's a challenge that scares me a bit," said Jim. "You *Warblers* will certainly be in demand for future gigs because of your notoriety. Or the firebug's notoriety.

"And to top all, the Iowa State Fair in Des Moines, one of the biggest in the country, wants to add the *Warblers* to the line-up. Maybe with a sing-along. Think you can sape them up, Marla?"

"Hafta see that *State Fair* movie again to get in the spirit of that big Iowa event," chuckled Marla.

"By the way," added Jim, "you can learn more about show biz from another Dane who will be on the marque—pianist-comedian Victor Borge.

"He mixes humor into his commentary and music with great skill.

"So, Marla, can you prepare them for the big time?" asked Jim.

"Well," responded Marla, "I can seek help from my alma mater in Des Moines, Grand View College, where I got my two-year degree before departing for Juilliard. I'm a part-time adjunct professor there as well as at the University of Iowa in Iowa City. Should be able to tap into some helpful resources.

"Besides, I may have a new collaborator to help with music. Got time for another challenge, William?" asked Marla.

Startled...then with delayed enthusiasm, he piped up, "That would be a great way to wind up work on my Master's Degree... especially benefiting from your wide involvement in music. It happens to tie in with my Scandinavian roots as well, though make mine Swedish!" he laughed.

Meridith Willson

"Look out Meridith Willson! I learned a lot about you at Juilliard," exclaimed Marla, "so watch our expanding team of mentors prepare the *Warblers* for creative warbling!"

Everyone else then grinned as William hugged Marla.

To wind up the gathering, Annicka offered take-home food as Jim and the three *Warblers* decided to leave, after they exclaimed about the wonderful concert—with appreciation overflowing for Marla.

"We're all sorry about the burning of the Christmas tree," she reminded them. "But otherwise we and the folks from the church, school and community can feel a sense of accomplishment and enjoyment."

"Any sign of Quasimodo during or after the concert?" asked Jim.

"The constables and some helpers from school searched high and low, without a sniff of him," answered Marla. "I guess he lives in a hut hidden in a ravine near the highway but well concealed from traffic, according to one of the constables.

"Well, that reminder does frighten me a bit," she added. "So William, will you take me back to my humble quarters?"

"At your service," grinned William. "Quasimodo won't scare me when I'm with you," he laughed, along with the others.

Krag and Kay smiled as they made good use of the considerable time William was gone.

"Sorry for the delay," apologized William when he returned. "We finally had time to talk about music."

"Okay, lover—I mean music lover, time for us to hit the lonesome trail," smiled Kay. "At least I will be lonesome, and I suspect you will be too."

"And I know I will be," said Krag, as he hugged and kissed Kay—right in front of William.

"Hope we didn't embarrass you, William, but you had your chance with Marla."

"I know…and I took it," he said, as he blushed.

"No snow in the forecast," Krag reported, as he accompanied Kay and William to Kay's Mustang.

"With good weather, you should enjoy a pleasant drive home.

"I'll miss you," he said, "a lot!" as he opened the door for Kay. And kissed her before she got in the car.

She wiped her eyes with a tissue, and explained: "Can't drive with my eyes fogged over."

"Tell Frank that I'll examine the drawings carefully and jot down my thoughts for us to talk about," said Krag. "Good excuse to see you again," he smiled. And so did she.

For several minutes after the Mustang disappeared, he stood with his hands in his pockets.

Staring without looking.

Mustang

A week later, the firebug's postcard arrived, like clockwork:

Candle and wick in bottle of gasoline lit Christmas torch for your torch. Quasimodo!

Jim, the Postmaster, the constables, Marla and the *Warblers* convened at the post office, again.

"The grapevine must be working," said Marla, "because now the firebug knows our Quasimodo label. The reference to your 'torch,' Krag, seems like an ongoing threat to you—through Kay. Maybe to her too, if Quasimodo decides to branch out. A scary possibility!"

"Sure is," Krag agreed loudly. "I'll alert Kay to be ever more vigilant. No predicting this bird."

During a period of quiet, the *Warblers* prepared for a new challenge—Christmas music.

So Marla suggested some easy carols, with a spiritual message, "because you'll be singing at our church as well as in the school auditorium again. At least the music should help us get past the burning Christmas tree and focus on a new one."

Krag called Kay to invite her to the Christmas event—and to seek her reactions to the latest postcard. Reluctantly, she expressed her regrets, as she explained her obligation to visit her family in Canute.

"They're eager to have me come again. I think they can't wait to learn the progress of my modern romance."

"Well, a skinflint in my family heard about my romance and called to worn me to guard my pocketbook," said Krag. "And to beware at my age of being taken in by a cute young chick. Especially one with an economics degree."

"How, may I ask," responded Kay, "did you explain our romance?"

"I admitted that 'cute young chick' fits you," answered Krag, "because you are involved in agriculture in a major way. PhD in economics, too, so you know the nature of my 'nest egg' at KJ Industries."

"Thanks, I think, for calling me a cute young chick. All the better to take advantage of you, my dear," laughed Kay.

"I'm getting other pressure right here at the *Homestead*," explained Krag. "Annicka scolds me — saying that I should act on my obvious desire to be with you. And my friends at KRRL warn me not to miss a golden opportunity. Even got a push from Marla.

"I did explain to my clan that you would make a perfect fit for the *Homestead*," added Krag. "You could run the place with one hand tied behind your back while continuing your responsibilities at the University.

"By the way, I wonder, though, can a married woman be employed?" asked Krag. "I heard that in the Great Depression that wasn't allowed in many places, such as Iowa."

"Oh yes, I'm certain that restriction disappeared long ago," laughed Kay.

"Now you know the quickest route between here and Ames," said Krag, "so I suppose you could arrange with the University some sort of modified commuting schedule."

"Wait a minute!" countered Kay. "I've heard of subtle compliments, but did you just make a subtle proposal?"

"You are definitely smart as well as cute," teased Krag. "Subtle it may have been, because I'm not skilled at proposing. But, yes, I would like to marry you. And I'd like to have you marry me," he chuckled.

"Our pastor said he would be delighted to perform the wedding ceremony right here at our *Homestead*. Or in our church, if preferred. Or in Canute. Or at the University.

"I'm not fussy — except in the choice of my bride," added Krag.

"Wow! You do have a way of shocking a person—in a subtle way, of course. You did actually say marriage, didn't you?" exclaimed Kay.

"Yes."

"Then in answer, I say 'yes' as well," chuckled Kay. "And I'm not fussy about the place, either. The person, but not the place!

"And you, Krag, are the perfect person!"

Chapter 19: Shootout at OK Corral

In the barn at the *Homestead*, Krag wandered among his tractors and vehicles as he pictured himself in his glassed-in office. And he pictured himself happily married to Kay.

He leaned on his Fordson tractor and marvelled at its restored beauty. Like he marvelled at the mature beauty of Kay. In an impulse of enthusiasm, he got the Fordson ready for action and cranked the engine.

After it roared to life, he climbed on and drove it out into the yard to perform some unneeded chore.

Just as he leaned over to attach a cable to a rock sled, he heard a sound from behind.

"Well, well, we meet again," said a distantly familiar voice. "Yah, I'm Quasimodo, as some of the folks, including your friends, call me. This time I've got the upper hand," he said, as he pointed his Luger at Krag. "Yah! Remember me, from Lake Michigan?"

"Now I do, when I hear your German sound," answered Krag. "You're Hans Schreiber and you tried to drown me in an underwater Navy exercise. We found out that you were a Nazis deserter, but claimed to be Danish so you could escape to America."

"Yah, I'm from Holstein, so I could speak Danish as well as German. And now I can act like Quasimodo to fool everyone.

"After I escaped from that secured farm holding German prisoners, I worked my way into this Danish community. Then I learned about you and your family farm and saw my chance for long-overdue revenge."

"Revenge, against me?" shouted Krag. "When you tried to kill me!"

"Yah, I learned later the term for what you and your Navy buddies did to me. Keel-haul, it's called, when you dragged me behind your boat, under the water half the time, until I nearly drowned."

"We could have shot you because you tried to murder me, but you survived your water ride, you bastard," hollered Krag.

"Now I could shoot you," said Quasimodo "but you have your tractor and cable ready to go, so instead I'll keel-haul you through a plowed-field. You'll learn how it feels!"

Fordson

Then as Krag stood by the tractor, Scheider hit him on the side of his head with the Luger. Next, he quickly tied Krag's hands and feet with short lengths of rope he had brought along. Then he hooked the cable from the Fordson to the rope around Krag's hands.

"Let's go plow a field!" bellowed Quasimodo as he started back toward the Fordson.

But a shout from behind stopped him in his tracks. "Don't move a muscle, and drop your gun," shouted Annicka.

"Drop it, or I'll drop you right now!" Annicka hollered again.

"You think you can stop me with that antique Danish peashooter," Quasimodo taunted.

"I can hit pheasants on the run or on the fly, so I'm sure I can hit you," answered Annicka. "Double barrels too!"

"Oh yah, stop me with your birdshot!" he taunted her once more.

So she warned, "I've got a bead on you, so drop your gun—or expect a load of this birdshot!"

When he started to raise his Luger, she pulled the trigger and a stream of bird shot followed the deafening sound of the shotgun.

He dropped the Luger as he went down, bellowing "You bitch, you hit me!"

"Remember, it's double-barrelled, so I've got another shot ready," she growled as she moved forward and kicked his pistol away from him—while pointing her shotgun at his head.

Though still half-stunned, Krag unhooked himself from the cable and untied his feet, and Annicka untied his hands.

He picked up the Luger and kept it ready while he used the ropes from his hands and feet to tie up the dazed and bleeding Hans.

"Thanks, thanks Annicka," gushed Krag. "Now, please, go call the constable while I guard Quasimodo with your shotgun and his Luger."

"I'm on my way," she declared with vigor. "Here's another shell to replace the one I fired," she said as she tossed the shell to Krag.

Within minutes, Annicka came back as the rare sound of a police siren echoed against the barns. Two constables jumped out of their car and joined Krag in covering Hans.

In a few more minutes, Steve and Marla arrived, followed a short time later by Harry and Mike. Then Jim arrived with his mobile broadcast system, awaiting his chance for a report.

Before the constables drove off with their manacled and bandaged prisoner, they stayed briefly to gather information.

Then Jim recorded Annicka's rambling crime description, as her shrill voice added to the drama of the scene.

After the constables left with Scheider in the police car, the others gathered in the *Homestead* kitchen, while Jim headed to KRRL to broadcast the breaking news.

While they talked about the series of fires and threats by the firebug and now the shooting, Annicka brewed coffee and warmed up *aebelskiver*.

Marla answered when the phone rang a half-hour later, and she called Krag to the phone to alert him that "a greatly worried but relieved Kay is on the line."

"We heard on the radio about the wild shoot-out at the *Homestead*," said Kay, in a tensed voice. "I'm so relieved that you're okay—just when you've added love and zest to my life. Oh, what a terrifying experience that must have been for you and Annicka!

"This terrible threat makes me realize all the more how deeply I love you, Krag."

"And it really focused my love for you, Kay!" said Krag.

Then with a quaver in his voice, he added, "When Quasimodo waved his pistol around, I was terrified that I'd never see you and hold you again. But now I will!"

The end of the beginning